D0564016

Texas Country Singers

Texas Country Singers

by **Phil Fry**
and **Jim Lee**

TCU PRESS • FORT WORTH
A TEXAS SMALL BOOK ★

Fry, Phillip L.
  Texas country singers / by Phillip L. Fry and James Ward Lee.
-- 1st ed.
    p. cm.
  ISBN 978-0-87565-365-5 (alk. paper)
  1. Singers--Texas--Biography. 2. Country musicians--Texas--
Biography. I. Lee, James Ward. II. Title.
  ML400.L435 2008
  782.421642092'2764--dc22
  [B]
                                    2007038863

TCU Press
P. O. Box 298300
Fort Worth, TX 76129
817.257.7822
http://www.prs.tcu.edu

to order books: 800.826.8911

Cover photo courtesy of Phil Fry.
Design: Margie Adkins Graphic Design

Dedication

For Barbara Bordelon and Diane Dodson

We Waltzed Across Texas

Contents

Introduction

Before anybody gets worked up, we know a lot of great Texas singers are missing from these pages, but "we have our reasons," as they say in war movies. But, hey, we have space limitations, and we have to have some rules here! We left out some great singers, some we like immoderately. For instance, two of our favorite singers are Stan Alexander and Francis Edward Abernethy, the two lead singers of "The East Texas String Ensemble" (pronounced "Insimble"). And we left out Kenneth Threadgill, a greater yodeler than Jimmie Rodgers and a pretty fair country singer and filling station operator. We did not include another favorite of ours, Gary P. Nunn, who wrote the newest Texas anthem "London Homesick Blues," ("I want to go home with the Armadillo/Good country music from Amarillo and Ab-o-leene. . ."). It distressed us to leave out the late Hoyle Nix ("Big Balls in Cowtown") and his son Jody.

If you are wondering why Bob Wills is not in this book it is because he was not a singer. We know, we know! ("When you're down in Texas, Bob Wills is still the king.") But he wasn't a singer. Maybe he sang a little bit in his early days, but all the great Bob Wills' songs are sung by someone else—Tommy Duncan or Mel Tillis or Milton Brown or Leon Rausch or Tag Lambert, who doubled as his driver. Needless to say, we do include Tommy Duncan and Milton Brown, but Leon was born in Missouri and Mel Tillis in Florida. And in case you haven't figured it out, all our singers were born in Texas. You can see where our state-line rule hammers us. We were sure at one point that we would include Ted Daffan of Ted Daffan's Texans, but, sad to say, he was from Louisiana.

Some we excluded for various odd reasons. We both used to love dancing to Al Dean and the All Stars (not with each other let us hastily add), but we can't find anything on Al Dean—not even in the great Bill C. Malone's *Country Music, USA*. We see some album covers for Al Dean, but no biography anywhere. He could be from Fort Worth for all we know. Or Muskogee, Oklahoma, where Merle Haggard is not from. No, Mighty Merle was born in Bakersfield, California, where he stole away Texan Buck Owens' wife, Bonnie.

Now we come to the hard part, the part where we tell the artists we almost included but didn't for one reason or another. We studied hard on Dale Evans, from Uvalde, but decided that she was a western singer and movie star and not really country. (Go ahead, argue!) We left off Kenneth Threadgill because he never really got outside the region. We didn't demand that our singers make it to the Opry or the Louisiana Hayride or the National Barn Dance in Chicago or the Ozark Jamboree, but we didn't think singers who didn't stray far from home or make it big on major labels or hit the airwaves big time could make our cut. We must have called them "Regional," one of the nasty buzz words to denigrate writers and painters and singers no matter how good they were. Or are. That is why we didn't include Francis Abernethy and Stan Alexander, both as good as anybody who ever made it to the Opry. That is why we didn't include Steve Fromholz, whose "Texas Trilogy" is a classic—a regional classic. And why you don't see entries for Hoyle and Jodie Nix or Alvin Crow or Gary P. Nunn or B. W. Stevenson. We almost included Gary P. Nunn, but then we found very little on him in the various encyclopedias and web sites that would give us a full portrait. We also pondered including Red River Dave McEnery, Jimmy Dean (he of sausage fame), or Boxcar Willie from Sterrett, Texas (No, we didn't cut him just because he had a place in Branson). We almost wrote about Texas Ruby, but the biography was slight. We both like to listen to Delbert McClinton—and we have to admit that he is almost country in some songs—but deep down he is a rocker. We didn't include Dallas' Michael Martin Murphey because he went western instead of country, and we left out Red Steagall, a Texas poet laureate and western singer of some note.

We are not sure how to defend the ones we did include, though most fit anybody's category of Texas country. By that we mean traditional country and not rockabilly or what someone has called "hat acts," where performers put on western attire and come close to country before drifting off into rock or something that almost sounds country. Lyle Lovett and Robert Earl Keen may fall into what someone described as marking "a link between underground cowboy music and alternate country." One never has to apologize for including Willie and Waylon and Ernest Tubb. But we wondered awhile about adding Rhodes Scholar Kris Kristofferson, known mainly as a songwriter and movie actor, but some of his recording with Willie and Waylon and the Boys decided us.

We are sorry that we didn't have space for many more that we haven't apologized for above: Arky Blue from Bandera, Bill Boyd (though he was one of the great instrumentalists and not best known as a singer. Remember his "Under the Double Eagle" and "Lone Star Rag"?). We left out Clay Walker from Beaumont, Billy Walker, who does show up on the Opry, and Charlie Walker, also on the Opry, but more famous as a disc jockey than as a singer, even though "Pick Me up on Your Way Down" is as country as it gets. Who knows? Somebody may wonder why we didn't include Roy Orbison, who started out as country but wound up as something far different. Like Joe Ely, he is a flatland rocker. Then there is Mac Davis, who almost went country and then faded. Jimmy Dale Gilmore has some great songs that just miss being country. We left out Guy Clark on the basis that he is more a songwriter than a singer, though that may not be fair, and the same is true of Billy Joe Shaver, who sang and wrote and shot somebody in the face. Jeannie C. Riley is from Anson, but, let's face it, she had only one song, "Harper Valley P.T.A." And while we are in the Rs, we definitely left out Kenny Rogers from Houston, whose career ran from The First Edition to one fine song, "You Picked a Fine Time to Leave Me, Lucille, with Four Hundred

Children and a Crop in the Field" (or that's what it sounded like). We know when to "hold 'em and when to fold 'em." Luckily for us, Lee Ann Rimes was born in Mississippi or we would have her partisans "Blueing" all over us. We might have considered Tracy Byrd and Mark Chestnut and Rodney Crowell, but we didn't. Sue us. Freddy Fender has one song that almost passed for country—"Wasted Days and Wasted Nights"—but he

Top: The Broken Spoke in the early days. Courtesy of James White.
Bottom: Willie Nelson and James White at the Broken Spoke. Courtesy of James White.

was a conjunto rocker who named himself after a solid-body guitar (his real name was Baldemar Huerta).

If there were any justice in the world, we should have devoted several pages to Cindy Walker, though, as far as we know, she never sang a note. All she did was write some of the best country songs ever to top the charts, both pop and country. Where would we all be if it weren't for "When My Blue Moon Turns to Gold Again," "Cherokee Maiden," "You Don't Know Me," "Bubbles in My Beer," and Roy Orbison's "Dream Baby." And maybe we should have written a lot about James White, who has kept the Broken Spoke in Austin running as a great honky-tonk. James has at one time or another included everyone from Ernest Tubb to Willie to Merle Haggard (not from Muskogee) to the late Don Walser from Lamesa, Texas. In the great list of Broken Spoke performers are also Bob Wills, Hank Thompson, Floyd Tillman, and one of our all-time favorite groups, Aubrey "Blue" Lowden. James White deserves some serious credit so we are putting his Spoke on the cover.

We owe more debts than we can pay properly. David Morris of Liberty Hill spent a whole afternoon telling us more about Jim Reeves than anybody else in the country knows. And then there is the head of the Jim Reeves Fan club Arie den Dult from Holland, who gave us photos and a complete set of newsletters. We obtained Ray Price photos from Sandra Orwig at his fan club, and we have one photo from the camera of Lyndol Fry of Hugo, Oklahoma, former Game and

Fish Commissioner of the Sooner State. We owe a debt to the great bassist of the old Threadgill band, Chuck Joyce of Babylon, New York, who was on the Austin scene when Phillip Fry and Jim Lee danced their "shoe heels round as apples" with Barbara Bordelon and the late Diane Dodson, to whom we dedicate this book. ★

Gene Autry

Orvon Grover Autry was born in Tioga, Texas, September 29, 1907, and died in Los Angeles, California, October 3, 1998.

Autry is not remembered as a country singer today, mostly because of his hugely successful career in movies as the "Singing Cowboy." His first big hit, "That Silver-Haired Daddy of Mine," was a country song that sold a million copies and set an industry record for sales. When it was put on an album, it became the first album in history to go gold. So whatever Autry's appeal to an entire generation growing up on western movies where the premise was "have a little action, sing a little song, jump on a horse and ride" (with most of the bad guys driving cars and talking on the telephone), he was the consummate singer, songwriter, actor, and later businessman. Autry was not only a singer of great fame, he was a prolific songwriter.

Autry's family moved to Oklahoma when he was still a small child, and he first performed in his grandfather's church choir. He later learned to play the guitar on a $12 Sears mail-order model and began picking and singing at local events. In his teens he got a job as a relief telegraph operator, where he was eventually "discovered" by Will Rogers, who encouraged him to go to New York City. He was advised to hit all the record companies with his own interpretations of Gene Austin and Al Jolson hits. He did test records for Edison and Victor, but there was no steady work in recording or radio for him. He left for Tulsa, Oklahoma, where he spent 1928–1929 on KVOO singing mostly Jimmie Rodgers hits and billing himself as "Oklahoma's Yodeling Cowboy." He returned to New York City about the time of the great market crash and managed to record for the next two years, mostly commercially marketed versions of his Jimmie Rodgers hits. "That Silver Haired Daddy of Mine" was recorded as a duet with Jimmy Long, and this success propelled Autry to Chicago and WLS, where he began to develop his western songs and where he adopted the cowboy attire that he was to wear to the end of his life.

In 1934, Autry drove to California, accompanied by another of his radio troupe, Lester "Smiley" Burnette, and that year Autry appeared in the movie *In Old Santa Fe;* the next year he began his own series, a science-fiction serial, *The Phantom Empire,* and soon he was the number-one box-office attraction in western movies. This period of Autry's career spawned a number of hit records that verged on popular music but somehow appealed to his country audience as well:

"Tumbling Tumbleweeds," "Mexicali Rose," "Take Me Back to My Boots and Saddle," "South of the Border," "Back in the Saddle." He played himself in the movies or perhaps a version of what the audience thought Gene Autry was. He was the good guy who can outwit and out-sing nearly anyone, and he was not too mushy with the girls. He was not a superhero, but he was not the Lone Ranger either. His character was someone who liked a good joke, usually on or by his sidekick Smiley Burnette. Autry continued his radio work, interrupted by three years as a transport pilot in the army air corps in World War II.

Gene's *Melody Ranch* broadcast was a long-running success for CBS, ending only in 1956. Autry saw the new medium of television as yet another outlet for him, and *The Gene Autry Show,* produced by his own Flying A Productions debuted in July of 1950 and lasted for six years.

Autry was an astute businessman who accumulated a fortune through investments in real estate, radio, television, publishing, and recordings. His popularity as a western cowboy was not dimmed by the pop hits that sold millions of records: "Here Comes Santa Claus," "Rudolph, the Red-Nosed Reindeer," "Peter Cottontail," and "Frosty the Snow Man." He produced his own feature films from 1947 through 1953. By the late 1950s Autry was looking for other ventures, and in 1960 he purchased the Los Angeles Angels baseball team (now the Anaheim Angels). He was inducted into the Country Music Hall of Fame in 1969, the Nashville

Songwriters Hall of Fame in 1970, the Texas Country Music Hall of Fame in 1998, and the Radio Hall of Fame in 2003. Before he died at age ninety-one, he had amassed an unprecedented five stars on the Hollywood Walk of Fame. His autobiography, *Back in the Saddle Again,* was published in 1978. Following the death of his first wife, Ina Spivey, Autry married Jackie Ellam in 1981. ★

Milton Brown

Born William Milton Brown in Stephenville, Texas, September 8, 1903; died in Fort Worth, April 18, 1936.

Milton Brown emerged for a brief time as the most promising musician to come out of Texas. His roots were country, but his singing style was blues and jazz as much as country, with popular, folk, and western thrown in for good measure. He is credited, for good reason, as a band leader who got people dancing to all kinds of rhythms and sounds, and he seemed not to care about the origin of the tune: if he could make them dance, he could get a crowd. He only recorded about 100 songs, but to read the discography is to see early influences on Bob Wills and on many later crooners, rockabilly types, and pure country singers from Elvis Presley to Willie Nelson.

Brown's parents were cotton sharecroppers, but Milton and his sister, Fay Era, were spared the toils of the fields, both attending school and singing from a young age. He entertained early at a place called the Stephenville Jokey Yard, where traveling medicine shows and itinerant musicians performed. His brother, Melvin Durwood, was born in 1915, but his sister Era died three years later. The family moved to Fort Worth, where his brother Roy Lee Brown was born. Milton worked and attended school alternately and did not graduate from Fort Worth's Arlington Heights High School until 1925, when he was twenty-two years old. He was apparently in Fort Worth for the next two years and may have done some singing, because by 1927 he was singing in a Fort Worth group called The Rock Island Rockets. His younger brother Durwood showed up with Milton, playing guitar, and in 1930 the brothers met fiddler Bob Wills and guitarist Herman Arnspiger at a house dance in Fort Worth. This meeting led to the formation of The Wills Fiddle Band, and they began appearing on radio and in such local venues as the Eagles' Fraternal Hall and the Crystal Springs Dance Hall in far west Fort Worth. The band added new members Clifton "Sleepy" Johnson and Jesse Ashlock and began advertising Light Crust Flour for W. Lee O'Daniel of Burrus Mills. The Light Crust Doughboys were extremely successful, but O'Daniel clamped down on the dance hall gigs for the band, and Brown left. He formed his own group, the now legendary Musical Brownies, in 1932, adding several important members who helped him change the makeup of country and western music almost on a parallel track with Bob Wills and His Texas Playboys (Wills had also left the O'Daniel group). Both bands played an ever widening circle around Fort Worth, with Wills locating first in Waco and then in Tulsa, and their audiences grew as well. The Musical Brownies recorded before the Playboys, although Wills and Brown had recorded a few songs with the Doughboys. In 1934, Bob Dunn, steel guitarist, joined Brown's group, and in 1935 Cliff Bruner, a fiddler who was to make a name for himself in Texas music, joined the group.

The popularity of Western Swing, as it came to be called, was fueled at first by the three groups that often included many of the same players: The Light Crust Doughboys, which continued after 1931 and is still going today; The Musical Brownies; and The Texas Playboys, which under various labels continues to this day, although with fewer "original" Playboys who were with Wills while he was alive. Milton Brown, who Bob Wills said had "the finest voice I'd ever heard," may have stumbled upon the formula for Western Swing almost by accident, but given his musical talent, he may have been just lucky enough to have found instrumentalists who were so perfect together that the driving rhythms behind his smooth vocals could move from jazz to blues to minstrel to ballads and folk. Dunn's guitar was probably the first to be amplified; this changed everything. Unlike Wills' Western Swing bands, which included horns, the Musical Brownies used only fiddles, guitars, and a banjo. The recordings were usually done in one take, and one recorded live broadcast on WRR in 1932 caught the band members wisecracking after they wound up "Hallelujah." A typical dance by Brown's band would include such incongruous titles as "Somebody Stole My Gal," "The Sweetheart of Sigma Chi," "Where You Been So Long, Corinne?," "The Sheik of Araby," "Bring It On Down to My House, Honey," "When I Take My Sugar to Tea," "Goofus," "Easy Ridin' Papa," "I've Got the Blues for Mammy," and the band's theme song, "Fall in Line with the NRA," which in those days was not the National Rifle Association but the National Recovery Act, passed by Congress to bring the nation out of the Great Depression.

Sometimes a "shouter" in his delivery and sometimes a crooner or almost a gospel singer, Brown seemed headed for national prominence. He had married Mary Helen Hames in 1934, and they had a son, but she did not like his untraditional, traveling lifestyle, and they divorced in 1936. In April of 1936 Brown was returning from Crystal Springs and another Fort Worth nightspot and evidently fell asleep at the wheel, killing a young female passenger and sending him to Methodist Hospital, where he died of pneumonia. Accounts of his funeral say that perhaps 3,500 people attended. In a few brief years of performance and recordings, Brown was not only an influence on later generations of fans and musicians, and not only rightfully called the Father of Western Swing, but he may forever have changed the landscape of "country" music derived from Appalachian, folk, minstrel, and songs in the southern tradition blended with jazz. Sadly, Milton Brown has not been inducted into any of the halls of fame that feature country and western singers, but he has had a scholarly biography devoted to his life and works. It is by Cary Ginell and entitled, appropriately, *Milton Brown and the Founding of Western Swing* (University of Illinois Press, 1994). ★

Johnny Bush

*John Bush Chinn III was born in Houston on
February 17, 1935.*

His greatest fame comes from a song he wrote rather than from a string of famous country hits he sang. In 1972, he wrote and recorded "Whiskey River," which for the last thirty-five years has become Willie Nelson's theme song and probably his biggest hit.

Early in life, Johnny Chinn was much taken by the music of all the Texas greats: Bob Wills, Ernest Tubb, Lefty Frizzell, and Hank Thompson. He sang for

Johnny Bush.
Courtesy of Shilah Morrow.

a time on station KTHT in Houston, but in 1951, he moved to San Antonio to make a name for himself as a country singer and drummer. Once, when playing at the Texas Star Inn, the announcer made a mistake and introduced him as "Johnny Bush." The name stuck, and hardly anybody remembers John Chinn III as a name in country music. Johnny Bush fronted such groups as Mission City Playboys, The Texas Top Hands, and The Texas Plainsmen before moving to Nashville and joining Ray Price and The Cherokee Cowboys as a drummer in 1963. Ray's bass player at that time was Willie Nelson. Bush was perfectly in tune with Ray Price's 4/4 shuffle beat, and his drum work did much to help Price popularize that country sound.

When Willie Nelson formed a group called Willie Nelson's Record Men, Johnny went along and sang with the group. His first single, "Sound of a Heartache," came out in 1967. For several years he enjoyed modest success as a singer with songs like "You Gave Me a Mountain," and "I'll Be There." Some of his songs went to number one on the Texas charts and ranked in the top twenty on the national hit list. In 1972, he wrote and recorded "Whiskey River" and was on his way to stardom. Then his voice failed him, and for years Johnny Bush was only famous for having written the celebrated Nelson hit.

Johnny's voice lost much of its range, yet he tried for some years to sing despite his limitations. His promise as "the Country Caruso" seemed to dim. At first, he could not hit the high notes, and then he found himself unable to sing at all. At one point, he feared that he would not even be able to talk. Doctors checked for nodules and polyps on the vocal cords and found nothing. There did not seem to be anything organically wrong with his voice. Finally, he was diagnosed with spasmodic dysphonia, a disease that shuts down the vocal cords. At the time, there was no treatment for his malady, and he resigned himself to a career outside music. At the time, he decided that his illness was God's judgment for his adulterous life—he was cheating on his wife and his girlfriend at the same time, both of whom contemplated suicide.

Then, it was discovered that Botox injected directly into the throat could restore the voice, and Johnny Bush resumed his successful career as a singer. Johnny Bush records many of the travails of his life in his 2007 autobiography, *Whiskey River (Take My Mind): The True Story of Texas Honky-Tonk,* published by the University of Texas Press. Beginning in the mid-nineties, he began releasing a series of albums with Darrell McCall and other singers. He did a tribute album, *Johnny Bush Sings Bob Wills* in 2001, *Johnny Bush's Honkytonic* in 2004, *Texas State of Mind* in 2007, and his latest, *Kashmere Gardens Mud: A Tribute to Houston's Country Soul.* The title of that album recalls the section where he grew up in Houston, Kashmere Gardens, an area with unpaved streets in one of the poorer parts of town. That album includes many country standards made famous by the singers he grew up admiring, plus a few of his own. He sings the Moon Mullican hit, "I'll Sail My Ship Alone," and such favorites as "Born to

Lose," "Jole Blon," and Willie's famous "Bloody Mary Morning." Johnny Bush, voice now partially restored, tours with the likes of Willie and Merle Haggard. In 2003, he was inducted into the Texas Country Music Hall of Fame. In 2007, he performed at the Country Music Hall of Fame in Nashville in a program titled "The Country Caruso: The Artistry of Johnny Bush." At that performance, someone quoted Ray Price as saying, "I am as proud of Johnny Bush as I am of Willie Nelson, Roger Miller, and Johnny Paycheck—all Cherokee Cowboys alumni." ★

Vernon Dalhart

Born Marion Try Slaughter in Jefferson, Texas, on April 6, 1883; Slaughter/Dalhart died in Bridgeport, Connecticut, on September 15, 1948.

Dalhart's biography, by Jack Palmer, is titled *Vernon Dalhart: The First Star of Country Music,* but Dalhart's career ranges all over the musical map from Negro minstrels to light and grand opera to popular music of the teens and twenties to folk and topical songs. Grandson of a Ku Klux Klansman who later became a law officer in East Texas, Marion Try Slaughter punched cattle on the Texas plains as a teenager, and then, when his father was killed in a knife fight with brother-in-law Bob Castleberry (allegedly over Slaughter's mistreatment of Vernon's mother), young Marion Try and his mother moved to Dallas about

1898 where he studied at the Dallas Conservatory of Music and was a paid soloist at the First Baptist Church of Dallas. He married in 1901 (he fathered a daughter, Janice, and a son, Marion Try Slaughter III), moved to New York in 1910, and in 1911 landed what was called a principal minor role in Puccini's *Girl of the Golden West,* which toured the country for six months. For his program listing for *Girl,* he used the pseudonym Vernon Dalhart, a name he took from two Texas towns near where he punched cattle as a youngster. He sang a tenor role and toured in *Madame Butterfly* in 1912, and in 1914 sang the role of Ralph Rackstraw in Gilbert and Sullivan's *HMS Pinafore* in New York and toured with the company. He sang tenor roles in several other operas and operettas.

During a recording career that stretched from 1916 to 1939, he made thousands of records of all sorts. He used hundreds of pseudonyms partly because the record companies did not want his name on both their expensive (seventy-five cents) and cheap records (twenty-five cents). Jack Palmer thinks he used as many as 200 pseudonyms. He was alternately Val Veteran, Hugh Latimer, Al Craven, Tobe Little, Bob White, to name some of the better known ones. Dalhart sang some of the now-forgotten topical songs of the day: "The Death of Floyd Collins," "Little Marian Parker," and "The Trial of John T. Scopes." Between 1916 and 1923, he made over 400 records with the Edison Company. One of his early hits was a minstrel song called "Can't You Heah Me Callin', Caroline?" He also recorded "Golden Slippers," "Polly Wolly Doodle," and the famous World War I song "Till We Meet Again," a song which enjoyed a good deal of popularity during the Second World War. Between 1925 and 1930, Dalhart made more records than any singer in America. One of his hits of this era was "Home on the Range," Franklin D. Roosevelt's favorite song. He also recorded such westerns as "Bury Me Not on the Lone Prairie" and "When the Work's All Done This Fall."

From 1924 to 1928, he joined guitarist and songwriter Carson Robison, who has been called "the granddaddy of the hillbillies," and violinist Adelyne Hood. Dalhart sang and played the harmonica and Jews' harp on some of their recordings. By this time, Dalhart was almost solely country and western. It was during this period that Vernon Dalhart's "The Wreck of the Old '97" and "The Prisoner's Song" took the country by storm. These two songs were released as A and B sides of the same record and remained on the charts for months. "The Prisoner's Song" ("Oh, if I had the wings of an angel") was number one for twelve weeks. According to Dalhart's biographer Jack Palmer, writing in *The Handbook of Texas Music*, Dalhart recorded "The Prisoner's Song" on fifty labels and made it the biggest selling song of the 1920s. In 1998 it was named one of the songs of the century and won a Grammy Hall of Fame Award.

In 1931 Dalhart and Adelyne Hood did a radio show called *Barber Shop Chords* for Barbasol Shave Cream, but by this time his career as a country singer was waning when real "hillbillies" like the Carter Family and Jimmie Rodgers were making hit records and getting airtime on country stations. Dalhart lost much of his money following the stock market crash of 1929, and his career faded during the thirties, his last recording being made in 1939. He spent the war years as a night watchman in a defense plant and ended his life as a night baggage clerk at Barnum's Hotel in Bridgeport, Connecticut, where he died of a heart attack. He is buried in Bridgeport under a stone that mentions both the Slaughter and the Dalhart name.

Vernon Dalhart was inducted into the Nashville Songwriters Hall of Fame in 1970, the Country Music Hall of Fame in 1981, and the Texas Country Music Hall of Fame in 1995. Unfortunately, Jack Palmer's *Vernon Dalhart* is out of print. ★

Tommy Duncan

Thomas Elmer Duncan was born on January 22, 1911 in Whitney, Texas, and died in San Diego, California, on July 25, 1967.

The lead vocalist during the heyday of Bob Wills' Texas Playboys, Tommy Duncan was a versatile singer who fitted perfectly into the blend of blues, swing, jazz, and country music that Wills wanted people to dance to. Duncan worked the fields his family tended as truck farmers, often alongside blacks who would influence his singing later, a background he had in common with

Bob Wills. He was greatly influenced by the recordings of Jimmie Rodgers. By age seventeen he was on his own, later going broke on a leased farm near Hedley. In 1930 he was in Amarillo broadcasting on WDAC but shortly left for Fort Worth, where he scraped by playing guitar and piano (self taught, no doubt) and apparently playing with a band led by Arnie Armstrong for several years before auditioning for Wills in 1932.

Bob Wills was working for W. Lee O'Daniel's Lightcrust Doughboys, largely promoting Lightcrust Flour from Burrus Mills in Fort Worth. Duncan had been asked by Wills to sing "I Ain't Got Nobody" for the audition, and this selection tells a lot about the influences on both men, since the song had been recorded by Bessie Smith and Emmett Miller and could be either pure New Orleans jazz or more of a blues song. Duncan beat out sixty-six other contestants after Wills had spent most of the night listening to him. Wills was on a collision course with O'Daniel, and when Wills left the Lightcrust Doughboys, Duncan stayed with Wills for the next fifteen years. Charles Townsend in Wills' biography, *San Antonio Rose*, says Duncan told Wills, "You hired me, O'Daniel didn't. And I'm not leavin' you until you do fire me. Anywhere you go I'm goin.'"

Bob Wills and
The Texas Playboys.
Courtesy of James White.

21

First settling in Waco, the band was soon named the Texas Playboys and was on the radio and playing dances all over the surrounding counties, but Wills was soon given a bigger chance in Tulsa, Oklahoma, after fighting a lawsuit brought by O'Daniel. Tulsa was to be the hub of the Texas Playboys for many years, the band taking different shapes and styles, going Hollywood, and for a while offering several bands in different locations.

Through their recordings, with Duncan as vocalist, the Playboys were reaching ever-widening audiences. The one song that put them out front was "New San Antonio Rose," an old fiddle tune that several Playboys contributed lyrics to. The song was recorded in Dallas in 1940 and sold three million recordings before Bing Crosby took his version to a second gold record.

Duncan volunteered for the armed services soon after the bombing of Pearl Harbor, and rejoined Wills in 1944 as the Playboys had stirred up interest in Hollywood with movies and personal appearances. Duncan was in such Wills movies as *Bob Wills and His Texas Playboys, Rhythm Roundup, Blazing the Western Trail, Lawless Empire*, and *The Frontier Frolic*. Duncan helped Wills write some new numbers, including "Stay a Little Longer," "Cotton-Eyed Joe," and "Sally Goodin." But Duncan's popularity, his own ego, and Wills' problems with the bottle, caused a split in 1948. Eldon Shamblin recalled that he got a call from Wills saying, "I can't stand to have that guy [Duncan] on the bandstand any more. I've reached my saturation point. I want you to fire him." "Bob, why don't you fire him?" Shamblin asked. Wills said, "He's no better than anyone else. You fire him. If I can't make it without him, it's time to quit." Shamblin told Wills, "Yeah. . . if you can't make it without him, I'd say it is time for you to quit."

Duncan formed his own group and named it Tommy Duncan and His Western All Stars. While the musicians were excellent and Duncan was in his prime, the band lasted only two years. It lacked the spark and spontaneity of the Playboys according to some, and even Duncan couldn't make up for not having Bob Wills on stage. The All Stars did some recordings, such as "Gambling Polka Dot Blues," "Sick, Sober, and Sorry," "Mississippi River Blues," and "Wrong Road Home Blues." After they disbanded, Duncan went on his own with personal appearances and recordings.

In 1959 Duncan reunited with the Wills band and for the next few years, on tour and in their recordings, the two were immensely popular. Their albums did better than ever: *Together Again, A Living Legend,* and *Mr. Words and Mr. Music* were made in 1960 and 1961, but soon after the two separated once again, with Duncan moving to California and Wills staying in Oklahoma and Texas. Duncan appeared with numerous bands on the West Coast for the next several years and died in San Diego in 1967. He influenced too many mainstream country and popular singers to mention, even though his style was neither pop, rock 'n roll, "Western," or pure country. His versatility matched perfectly the Western Swing style of the time. Duncan was one of the finest singers in country music, and it is mystifying that he has not been inducted into any of the halls of fame that many lesser singers have been honored by.★

Lefty Frizzell

Born William Orville Frizzell in Corsicana, Texas, March 31, 1928, and died in Nashville, Tennessee, July 19, 1975 (Buried on Music Row at Forest Lawn Cemetery in Goodlettsville, Tennessee).

In 1977, Willie Nelson released an album of the late Lefty Frizzell's songs called *To Lefty from Willie*. That was only one of the many tributes that poured in to honor the memory of one of the brightest stars of country music in the period between 1950 and 1975, the year of Lefty's death. Merle Haggard said of Lefty, "When I was fifteen, I thought Lefty Frizzell hung the moon . . . and I'm not sure he didn't."

Lefty Frizzell, the son of an oil-field roustabout, grew up in oil towns in Texas and Oklahoma and Arkansas. It was in Eldorado, Arkansas, in the late 1930s, that Lefty got his start playing on a children's program on radio station KELD. In 1945, when they were barely sixteen, Lefty met and married Alice Harper, and, in 1947 they set out, with their two-year-old daughter Lois, for Roswell, New Mexico, so that Lefty could try to make it as a radio singer for station KGFL and sing in some of the local servicemen's clubs. In Roswell

Lefty was arrested, according to a CMT biography, "for statutory rape" and sentenced to six months in jail. While in jail, he wrote love letters to Alice and sent her songs he was composing. One of the songs, "I Love You, I'll Prove It a Thousand Ways," became one of his great standards. He spent much of 1950 singing at the Ace of Clubs in Big Spring, Texas. Then, at age twenty-two, he landed a recording contract with Columbia Records. His career soared in the early fifties with a number of hit recordings.

In 1950, he joined the *Grand Ole Opry*. He was introduced by Red Foley on the *Opry's* famous *Prince Albert Show* and sang two of the songs for which he is best remembered—his love song to Alice written while he was in jail, "I Love You, I'll Prove It a Thousand Ways," and "I Want to Be With You Always." He was suddenly famous. At the *Opry*, he shared a dressing room with Hank Williams and then toured with him in 1951.

By 1952, when rock 'n roll was eroding some country stars' popularity, Lefty left the *Grand Ole Opry* and headed for California. He appeared as a regular on Cliffie Stone's TV show, *Hometown Jamboree*, and on a TV and radio show called *Town Hall Party*. In L.A. he played the Hollywood Bowl and clubs in the area. Despite a series of great hits like "Always Late," "I Want to Be with You Always," and "The Mom and Dad Waltz," his career was in the doldrums until he went to Nashville in 1959 and recorded "The Long Black Veil," a song by Danny Dill and Marijohn Wilkin. The song went to number one, and Lefty was back in business as a star.

In 1961, he moved back to Nashville to stay until his death in 1975. In 1963, he recorded "Saginaw, Michigan," another hit for him. Late in his career he recorded "I Never Go Around Mirrors," and "That's the Way Love Goes," both songs that have been featured by such stars as Merle Haggard and Willie Nelson.

At the height of his career, he had four songs in the top ten, a record not equaled until the Beatles surpassed it. During his short career, he had a total of thirteen top-ten songs, three of which reached number one.

Lefty was persuaded by the famous Hollywood tailor and designer Nudie Cohen to wear a suit with rhinestones. He was the first country singer to dress in the style that soon became a uniform for singers like Porter Waggoner and others.

He was inducted into the Nashville Songwriters Hall of Fame in 1972, and after his death was inducted into the Country Music Hall of Fame in 1982. He was inducted into the Texas Country Music Hall of Fame in 2003 and is one of the few country and western singers to have a star on the Hollywood Walk of Fame. His influence on other singers, in addition to Willie Nelson, Merle Haggard, George Strait, and George Jones is immense. His way of phrasing, of letting the notes slide, can be heard in many singers. He said of his vocal style, "I'm not really a lazy guy, but I get tired of holding a note for a long time. Instead of straining, I just let it roll out and it felt good to me."

Frizzell suffered from high blood pressure and alcohol addiction, and, instead of treating the hypertension, he simply increased his intake of alcohol. His death at age forty-seven shocked the country music world and left a void that has not been filled despite all the tributes by Willie Nelson and Merle Haggard and George Jones and his son Crockett Frizzell, who dedicated an album to *My Hero and My Father . . . Lefty Frizzell.* ★

Stuart Hamblen

Born in Kellyville, Texas, October 20, 1908, and died in Santa Monica, California, March 8, 1989.

Carl Stuart Hamblen is probably the only country singer ever to run for president of the United States. He ran on the Prohibition ticket in 1952 and came in fourth behind another Texas native, Dwight Eisenhower. The Prohibition Party got more than 78,000 votes, hardly enough to frighten Ike or the runner-up, Adlai Stevenson.

Hamblen's father was an itinerant preacher, and young Carl prepared himself to be a teacher before deciding to try his hand as a singer. He entered McMurry College in Abilene, Texas, and managed to get a spot singing on station KAYO in Abilene as a singing cowboy while still in school. His career as a teacher was over before it started, and he moved east to Dallas where he won a talent contest and headed to New York to try recording with RCA Victor. He made four records with RCA, one of which was his own composition, "The Big Rock Candy Mountain #2."

In 1930, he went to Hollywood and was a popular singer on the radio there for the rest of that decade. He formed a group with Patsy Montana, sang for a time with a locally popular group, The Beverly Hillbillies, and was a regular on radio station KFWB under various incarnations—*King Cowboy's Wooly West Review* and *Stuart Hamblen and His Lucky Stars* were two of his California shows.

In the 1930s Hamblen wrote a number of songs that became popular on country and western radio stations and on records. "My Mary," "Texas Plains," and "Ridin' Ole Paint," are the best known. Also, during the thirties and forties, Stuart Hamblen made several movies with such cowboy stars as Gene Autry, Roy Rogers, Don "Red" Barry, Bob Steele, and John Wayne. He often played minor parts, but in Roy Rogers' *The Arizona Kid* (1939) he plays the villain Val McBride. In the film *In Old Monterey* (1939), with Gene Autry and Gabby Hayes, he plays a bugler when Gene is sent to Monterey to persuade the ranchers to give up their land for an army base.

Hamblen enjoyed great popularity in several fields in the 1930s and 1940s, but his career suffered from his drinking and gambling. He says of himself that he was "the original juvenile delinquent." Nevertheless he turned out many songs during this period. Two of the most famous are the novelty song, "I Won't Go Hunting with You, Jake, but I'll Go Chasing Women" and the very big hit, "Remember Me, I'm the One Who Loves You," recorded by both Dean Martin and Ernest Tubb.

In 1952, Stuart Hamblen attended one of Billy Graham's crusades and decided on the spot to devote his life to religion. He gave up cigarettes and whiskey, sold off his race horses, and, as he put it, "hit the sawdust trail." At a party at John Wayne's house, the Duke was hazing him about his conversion, and Hamblen said, "It's no secret what God can do." John Wayne told him that would make a great song title. Hamblen wrote the song, which has been a standard at revivals and church services ever since. Stuart Hamblen devoted himself to religion by starting a program called *The Cowboy Church of the Air,* a show which was nationally syndicated from the 1950s well into the 1970s.

After his conversion, Hamblen wrote his best known song. On a hunting trip in the Sierras, he came across the body of a prospector and turned the event into the song "This Ole House," which was a number-one hit in seven countries at the same time. Everyone, country and pop, recorded "This Ole House." It was a big hit for Jo Stafford, Bing Crosby, Red Foley, and, later, Elvis Presley on one of his gospel albums. It was voted the song of the year in 1954.

Stuart Hamblen wrote 225 songs, many of which are sung in honky-tonks as well as churches today. His "Open Up Your Heart and Let the Sunshine In" is a theme song for many gospel groups. Honors were heaped upon him during the later years of his life. He was inducted into Nashville's Songwriters Hall of Fame in 1970, and the Academy of Country and Western Music gave him its Pioneer Award for being the first "singing country and western cowboy in the history of broadcasting." He was given a star on the Hollywood Walk of Fame in 1976, and the Los Angeles City Council proclaimed Stuart Hamblen Day that same year. He was inducted into the Texas Country Music Hall of Fame in 2001.

He was married to Suzy Hamblen for fifty-five years. She and two daughters survived him. He died following brain surgery in February 1989. Billy Graham, whose crusade converted Hamblen, spoke at the funeral service at the Hollywood Presbyterian Church. He is buried in Forest Lawn Cemetery in Hollywood. ★

Adolph Hofner

Born in Moulton, Texas, on June 8, 1916,
and died in San Antonio, June 2, 2000.

His amazing career put him in the mainstream of country music in the purest sense of "country" because he blended central European polkas, waltzes, marches, mazurkas, and other folk tunes into a mélange of Western Swing, Spanish rhythms, standard country songs, and lyrics sung in his first language, Czech. He started out, however, with Hawaiian music, when he and his brother Emil ordered a ukulele from Sears after moving with the family to San Antonio. Hofner claims they smashed the ukulele getting it out of the box. The brothers then moved up to guitars, with Adolph on acoustic and Emil (always called "Bash" because of his shyness) on steel guitar. They were influenced by Jimmie Rodgers, Bing Crosby, Russ Columbo, and Rudy Vallee, but when Adolph heard Milton Brown and his Musical Brownies he was hooked: "That's what sold me on western music—because they had a band."

The boys played in clubs around San Antonio in a trio called The Hawaiian Serenaders, and their partner Simon Garcia taught Adolph Lorenzo Barcelato's "Maria Elena," later to be his first big hit. KTSA offered them a fifteen-minute segment but cut them off before they were halfway through, not the last disappointment Adolph was to experience in the music business.

The Hofner brothers joined a small group headed by Jimmie Revard in 1936, calling themselves Oklahoma Cowboys to make sure they weren't confused with Bob Wills and His Texas Playboys. They recorded with Revard, moved to Oklahoma with the band, but moved back to San Antonio, where Adolph, again sidelined by disappointments in the music business, worked briefly as a mechanic.

The next gig was with Tom Dickey and The Showboys and, while this did not last long (Adolph was fired for showing up late one day), the group did record Floyd Tillman's classic "It Makes No Difference Now" with Adolph on vocals. The next venue was Adolph Hofner and All the Boys, later "Texans" instead of "Boys," and then Adolph Hofner and the San Antonians, the name they are best remembered by. They recorded "Maria Elena" in February of 1942, and it made the national charts, followed the next year by

31

"Cotton-Eyed Joe," although they may not have been the first to record it.

Both recordings established a reputation that eventually led the group to California during the war years, a time when Hofner adopted "Dub" (or sometimes "Dolph") as his official performing name because of the fear and hatred of Adolph Hitler. Back in San Antonio by the late 1940s, another band name change was a little more permanent: The San Antonians became The Pearl Wranglers and were sponsored by Pearl beer. They performed for Pearl in South and Central Texas for the next fifty years. They recorded with various labels, including Imperial, Columbia, RCA, Decca, and Sarg, and their fellow musicians over the years included noted songwriter and performer Floyd Tillman and fiddler J.R. Chartwell. A favorite venue in San Antonio was The Farmer's Daughter, whose owner cautioned the dancers before each rendition of "Cotton-Eyed Joe" that the word "bullshit" would not be tolerated or he would send the band home and lock the doors. But if that indeed ever happened, the crowds came back.

The mixture of influences in Hofner's music can be seen in the titles of one CD collection: "Maria Elena," "Spanish Two-Step," "Alamo Rag," "South Texas Swing," "Cotton-Eyed Joe," "Starkovarna," "Strashidlo," "Dis Ja Liebe Spim," "Na Marjanse," and, to round out the volume, "Longhorn Stomp." His bands usually consisted of guitars, fiddles, drums, piano, and bass, but in their larger performances horns and accordions were added. As a vocalist, Hofner was often billed early in his career as the "Bing

Crosby of Country" and later as "The Dean of Country Bandleaders," "The Sultan of Swing," "The Prince of Polka," and "The King of South Texas Swing." ★

Waylon Jennings

*Waylon Arnold Jennings was born June 15, 1937,
and died on February 13, 2002.*

In the sixty-five years of his turbulent life, he was a disc jockey, rockabilly artist, a pure rock 'n roller, a television performer, and one of the most successful country singers of modern times. Born in Littlefield, Texas, Waylon dropped out of high school in the tenth grade, became a local disc jockey in his home town, and by age eighteen was working for station KLLL in Lubbock and beginning a friendship with the famed rock artist Buddy Holly. Holly helped produce Waylon's first record, "Jole Blon" in 1958. By that time Waylon was playing bass—on a temporary basis—with Buddy Holly's Crickets. He was with the band in 1959 when Holly, Richie Valens, and J. R. Richardson were killed in a plane crash in Iowa. Waylon was supposed to be on the flight but gave up his seat to Richardson, "The Big Bopper," who was suffering with a cold. Since Waylon's last words to Holly were the joking comment, "I hope your plane crashes," he suffered a bout of depression that lasted for the better part of a year.

In 1960, Waylon was in Phoenix, Arizona, fronting a rockabilly band called The Waylors, when country star Bobby Bare heard him and managed to help him get a recording contract with Trend Records. Nothing came of that, and in 1963, Waylon went to the West Coast and made some recordings with Herb Alpert's A&M records. Waylon moved to Nashville in 1965 and hooked up with Chet Atkins' RCA label. In his early years in Nashville, he roomed with Johnny Cash, with whom he had a long-term professional relationship. It was in Nashville that he had his first top-ten hit, "Walk on out of My Mind."

Nashville was not geared for the likes of the hard-living Jennings, and he hated the syrupy "Nashville Sound" that Atkins and others advocated in the time that traditional country music was thought to be too "hillbilly." In 1970, he made a move that led to his greatest success. He joined Kris Kristofferson and Willie Nelson and was soon to move from Nashville to Austin, Texas, where Nelson was promoting a new sound in country music. By 1972, Waylon and Willie and the Boys were riding high with what they called "the Outlaw sound." In 1973, they recorded the album *Honky-tonk Heroes,* with most of the songs by Texas singer/songwriter Billy Joe Shaver. In 1974, Waylon had two number-one hits and one number-two. In first place were "This Time" and "I'm a Ramblin' Man," and his number-two hit was "Rainy Day Woman." He was voted Male Vocalist of the Year by the Country Music Association in 1975. The following year, *Wanted! The Outlaws,* which featured Waylon, his wife Jessi Colter, Willie Nelson, and Tompall Glaser, went to number one on the pop charts. These years saw some of his songs—"Luckenbach, Texas," for example—become number-one hits. He won his second Grammy with Willie in 1978 for "Don't Let Your Babies Grow up to Be Cowboys." He had originally won a Grammy with the Kimberlys for "McArthur Park" in 1969.

From the time he joined Willie Nelson, with time out for bouts of cocaine addiction and other abuses, Waylon had a series of great successes. His 1977 album, *Ol' Waylon*, went platinum, and his recording with Willie of "Don't Let Your Babies Grow up to be Cowboys" was a number-one hit. In 1977, he was also arrested for cocaine use in Nashville. The next year, Waylon wrote and sang the title song for the television series *The Dukes of Hazzard* and did the off-screen narration. During the early- and mid-eighties, Waylon was sunk in a period of addiction, but in 1985, he, Willie, Johnnie Cash, and Kris Kristofferson came out with *The Highwaymen* album. Its title song became a number-one hit. And in 1989, Waylon Jennings passed the GED examination and finished the high school career he had abandoned so many years before in Littlefield. His autobiography, *Waylon,* was published in 1989, and, in true Jennings fashion, didn't pull many punches.

In 2001, Waylon Jennings was inducted into the Country Music Hall of Fame, but he refused to attend the awards ceremony, as he had many others, because he said, "music is not a pissing contest." He had been selected to the Texas Music Hall of Fame in Carthage in 1999 and was a member of the Nashville Songwriters

Hall of Fame. By the time of his election to the CMA Hall of Fame, he was suffering from serious diabetes. First he lost a leg, and then, in February of 2002, he succumbed to the disease. He was survived by his wife, Jessi Colter, whom he had married in 1969, and by six children from four previous wives. He is buried in Mesa, Arizona. ★

George Jones
Born in Saratoga, Texas, on September 12, 1931.

George Jones, "Old Possum," was born in the Big Thicket area of Texas and grew up in and around Beaumont, living in the "projects" and singing for spare change on the streets of Beaumont. At nineteen he married the first of his four wives, fathered a daughter, but was divorced within a year. After a hitch in the Marine Corps, Jones was back in East Texas singing where he could and hoping for a break. The break came in 1955 with "Why Baby Why," a song that still appears in his albums.

Jones became a star in country music beginning in 1959 with his novelty song "White Lightning." In the sixties, he was voted male vocalist of the year five times. In 1960, George Jones recorded an album in tribute to one of his great influences: *George Salutes Hank Williams.* Early in life, Jones idolized Roy Acuff, Hank Williams, and Ernest Tubb, and some of the vocal styles of all three can be seen in his music, but above all, what one hears in Jones is that unmistakable, unique voice that nobody else can imitate.

Jones married again in 1954, and this time the marriage lasted until 1968—not a record—but one of remarkable longevity for a man whose drinking habits had become legendary. Despite the habits that troubled him, the sixties were good years for Jones. He recorded some of his best songs: "Walk through This World with Me," "The Race Is On," "A Good Year for the Roses," and one of his greatest songs, "She Thinks I Still Care."

In 1969, George married Tammy Wynette, one of the real queens of country music. They stayed married only until 1975, but they recorded a number of songs and an album or two during and after their married years. George and Tammy sang "We're Not the Jet Set," "Golden Ring," "We're Gonna Hold On," and other songs that rose on the charts. The marriage was a stormy one, and the story is told of George riding a lawn mower to a local bar because Tammy had taken his car keys away. (That same lawn-tractor incident is supposed to have happened during his second marriage also.) George and Tammy were divorced in 1975, and George continued the lifestyle that almost killed him more than once. He was addicted to alcohol and cocaine, and yet, in 1980, he recorded what was voted in 1992 the greatest all-time country song, "He Stopped Loving Her Today." After he had recorded the song, he listened to it in the studio and said, "Nobody is going to buy that morbid son of a bitch," but buy it they did, and it led to his being named CMA vocalist of the year in 1980 and 1981.

In 1983, Jones married Nancy Sepulveda, the wife he credits with helping him to kick the cocaine and alcohol habit. Actually, he was not always on the wagon during the years after 1983, for in 1999, he wrecked his Lexus while under the influence of alcohol and was in a coma for ten days. Since that incident, George Jones has been clean and sober and has lived down the nickname he acquired in the worst days of his life. He is no longer "No Show Jones," though he has recorded a funny song under that title.

In 1992, George Jones was inducted into the Country Music Hall of fame, and in 1999, he won a Grammy for *Choices.* George has recorded two recent albums with Merle Haggard, a singer who admires George as much as George admires "the Hag." Their 2006 album is entitled *Kicking Out the Footlights,* which seems an appropriate title for two rough country singers, one an ex-addict and one an ex-con.

By 2007, George Jones has been a country singer for fifty-seven years and a member of the *Opry* for thirty-eight years. He has won all the major awards, has sung at Carnegie Hall, has had more songs on the country charts—167—than any other singer, has 143 top-forty hits and seventy-eight top-ten hits. Frank Sinatra once said of Old Possum, "He is the second greatest white singer alive." ★

Kris Kristofferson

One of the most versatile singers, songwriters, and actors in the world of Texas country music, Kris Kristofferson was born in Brownsville, Texas, on June 22, 1936.

His father was an air force major general, and Kris' family moved a great deal in his early years. He attended Pomona College in California, graduating with a BA degree in English, a Phi Beta Kappa key, and a Rhodes Scholarship. In college, he was a star athlete in rugby, football, and track and field. *Sports Illustrated* featured him in a "Faces in the Crowd" section as one of the country's most promising athletes. His athletic prowess followed him to Oxford's Merton College, where he not only received an MA in English literature but won his "blue" in boxing. While still at Oxford, *Time Magazine* wrote a glowing profile of the young scholar, singer, athlete in its April 6, 1959, edition. Kris Kristofferson has been in one limelight or another for most of his adult life.

Because of his singing and songwriting, the British J. Arthur Rank recording company signed him to a contract as a singer while still at Merton. Producer Paul Lincoln recorded him under the name of Kris Carlson, but he was not a success.

Kris joined the army and rose to the rank of captain as a helicopter pilot. He was all set, in 1965, to be assigned to West Point to teach literature when he resigned his commission and moved to Nashville to try his hand in the music business. He had a hard

time breaking in and spent half of his time as a jani-
tor in Columbia's recording studios. During this time,
he also worked as a helicopter pilot in Louisiana, flying
between the oil platforms in the Gulf and the mainland.
He says he wrote "Me and Bobbie McGee" in Louisiana and "Help Me Make It through the Night" on an oil
derrick in the Gulf.

He began having hits as a songwriter in the late
sixties. Roger Miller recorded "Me and Bobbie McGee"
in 1969. Kris hit it big in 1971 when his "For the Good
Times" became a number-one hit for Ray Price, and
"Sunday Morning Coming Down" went to the top of
the charts for Johnny Cash. It is said that he attracted
Cash's attention when he landed a helicopter in Cash's
yard with songs in hand. "For the Good Times" won the
Academy of Country Music Award's Song of the Year in
1971, and Cash's recording of "Sunday Morning Coming Down" was the song of the year for the competing
Country Music Association that same year.

Sammie Smith had a number-one hit with Kris'
"Help Me Make It through the Night" in 1971, and Kris
won a Grammy for the song. Also in 1971, Janis Joplin
(alleged to be romantically involved with Kristofferson)
had a million seller with "Me and Bobbie McGee." Kris
recorded an album, *Kristofferson*, in 1970 and *The Silver
Tongued Devil and I* in 1971, but neither of his albums
made the charts. Someone has suggested that his four-
pack-a-day smoking habit had such a rasping effect on
his voice that he was never destined to be a great soloist.

It was about the time of his greatest success as a

songwriter that he began a movie career that has lasted from the early seventies until today. He has appeared in some sixty-five movies, documentaries, and television shows. He is best known for *Blume in Love* (1973), *Pat Garrett and Billy the Kid* (1973), *Bring Me the Head of Alfredo Garcia* (1974), *Alice Doesn't Live Here Anymore* (1974), *A Star Is Born* (1976), the Dan Jenkins classic *Semi Tough* (1977), and *Lone Star* (1996). Kris even starred in the 2001 remake of Texas writer William Broyles, Jr.'s *Planet of the Apes*.

From 1973 until 1980, Kristofferson was married to the singer Rita Coolidge, and they won two Grammies as best duo of the year. His best years as a singer came when he hooked up with Willie Nelson, Waylon Jennings, and Johnny Cash as The Highwaymen. Kris' "Why Me," on the *Highwaymen* album went to number one on the charts in 1985. In 1984, Kristofferson and Willie Nelson made a movie, *Songwriter*, and Kris' *Music from the Songwriter* was a hit album.

Kris Kristofferson is probably better known as a songwriter/actor than a singer, but that did not keep him from being made a member of the Country Music Hall of Fame in 2004. He had already been made a member of the Nashville Songwriters Hall of Fame

Kris Kristofferson and Willie Nelson at the Broken Spoke. Courtesy of James White.

in 1977 and the Songwriters Hall of Fame in 1985. In 2003, he was inducted into the Texas Country Music Hall of Fame. He won the Johnny Mercer Award from the Songwriter's Hall of Fame in 2006. That same year, he released his first album in eleven years, *This Old Road*. In 2007, Kris received the Johnny Cash Visionary Award from Country Music Television. ★

Barbara Mandrell
Born in Houston, Texas, on December 25, 1948.

Barbara Mandrell was an accomplished musician by the age of eleven, when she performed on the pedal steel guitar for a music trade show in Chicago. Her father, a country guitarist, got her started on the accordion, and before she was a teenager, she could play accordion, bass, guitar, mandolin, pedal steel, sax, and Dobro.

When she was eleven, the family moved to Los Angeles and Barbara became a regular on *The Town Hall Party,* a radio and television show. A year later she was on ABC's *Five Star Jubilee,* which was broadcast from one of the minor centers of country music located in Springfield, Missouri. That same year Barbara toured with Johnny Cash and Patsy Cline. Cline said of the twelve-year-old pedal steel virtuoso, "she played just out of this world."

Barbara Mandrell, one of the most beautiful country singers, was Miss Oceanside at age sixteen. She married Kenneth L. Dudney, a drummer in The

Mandrell Family Band while still in her teens. The Dudneys now have three grown children and—unlike many musical marriages—are still husband and wife.

Barbara Mandrell toured Vietnam when she was twenty, and at about that time decided to move to Nashville, where she visited the *Grand Ole Opry* for the first time. She had her first top ten hit in 1971 when she recorded "Tonight My Baby's Coming Home." In 1972, she joined the *Opry*, and in 1973 had her first number-one hit, "Midnight Oil."

Strongly influenced by a diverse group of singers such as Brenda Lee, James Brown, Aretha Franklin, Dolly Parton, and Tammy Wynette, her music has often been called country-soul, and there are echoes of blues and rock. She even lists *Opry* comedian Minnie Pearl as one of her influences, and of course there is the strong influence of the Mandrell family, who got her started in show business and who were one of the acts she appeared with. She sang and played with The Mandrell Family, and, in 1979, appeared on television as *Barbara Mandrell and the Mandrell Sisters*, where she was joined by her sisters Louise and Irlene.

She was Country Music Association Female Vocalist of the Year in 1979 and again in 1981, CMA Entertainer of the Year in 1980. She was cited in the *People's Choice* Awards as Best All-Around Female Entertainer in 1982, 1983, 1985, and 1987. She won *Billboard's* Best Single of the Year for "Sleeping Single in a Double Bed" in 1979. Nashville's *Music City News* named her Female Vocalist of the Year, Musician of the Year, and called her

TV show *Barbara Mandrell and the Mandrell Sisters* the Best TV Series in 1982. She won a Grammy in 1984, won the Pioneer Award from the Academy of Country Music in 2001, was called one of the Forty Greatest Women of Country Music by CMA in 2002, and won CMA's Triple Crown Award in 2005.

In addition to her career as a country singer, Barbara Mandrell appeared as an actress in such TV programs as *Diagnosis Murder, Doctor Quinn: Medicine Woman,* and *Baywatch.* For a time, she was a regular on the daytime soap *Sunset Beach.* In 1999 she played the role of the ingénue's mother in a made-for-television thriller, *The Wrong Girl.*

Mandrell had a serious car wreck in 1984. She broke several bones and was discovered to be pregnant with her third child, who was born in 1985. For several years after her accident, she cut down on her singing and public appearances and devoted time to recuperation and the writing of her autobiography, *Get to the Heart: My Story* (1991). Much of her time in recent years has been devoted to her acting career. ★

Roger Miller

Roger Dean Miller was born in Fort Worth, Texas, January 2, 1936, and died in Los Angeles, California, October 25, 1992.

Miller might be hard to label as country were it not for a number of pure honky-tonk compositions and his association with some of the finest country musicians of his era. Not only that, he played a variety of instruments well enough to front for some of the bands he was associated with. His father died when Roger was a year old, and he was sent to live with an aunt and uncle in Erick, Oklahoma. His childhood was not a happy one, and he often escaped into music: he doted on the *Grand Ole Opry* and The Light Crust Doughboys on the radio. At age eleven, he was given a fiddle by Sheb Wooley, his brother-in-law. After the eighth grade, Miller tried his luck as a ranch hand and rodeo rider. Later, instead of going to jail over a stolen guitar, he says, he joined the army: "My education was Korea, Clash of '52." Along the way, and even in the army, Miller became proficient on the guitar, banjo, piano, fiddle, and drums.

Miller migrated to Nashville in the 1950s, and, in 1957, having befriended George Jones, they co-wrote "Tall, Tall Trees," which Jones released to little notice. In 1958, Roger joined Ray Price's Cherokee Cowboys. He wrote one of Price's big hits, "Invitation to the Blues," which went to number three and is still in the Price repertory. In 1959, Jim Reeves recorded Miller's "Billy Bayou," one of Reeves' early hits. Miller played in back-up bands for Minnie Pearl, played drums for Faron Young's group, and made the charts as a singer with "When Two Worlds Collide," co-written by Bill Anderson.

During these years, Miller met many of the songwriters and performers he would work with the rest of his life. In addition to the above, he became friends with Willie Nelson, Johnny Cash, Kris Kristofferson, Ernest

Tubb ("Half a Mind"), and Eddy Arnold ("The Last Word in Lonesome is Me"). But the years in Nashville, one of which he worked as a bellhop, were not entirely satisfactory, and in 1963 Miller pulled up stakes for California, where he had already appeared on *The Tonight Show* and *The Jimmy Dean Show*. With his RCA contract expiring, Miller was picked up by Smash Records, and the initial cuts made for his first album would make him a star for sure. "Dang Me" (1964) went to number one on the country charts and then crossed over to the pop charts. The next few years produced "Chug-a-Lug," "Do-Wacka-Do," "King of the Road," "Engine, Engine No. 9," "One Dyin' and A-Buryin'," "Kansas City Star," and "England Swings." Miller's jazzy style and humorous word play seemed for a time to take him out of the bedrock of country music, but this was the era of the Beatles and the Rolling Stones, and Miller was on top of the charts with strong contenders.

Andy Williams recorded "In the Summertime," written by Miller, and Williams put him in his TV show in 1965. This led to Miller's own variety show in 1966, but the show was cancelled, and he spent the last part of that decade performing in numerous venues but recording very little. He did, however, record the first version of Kristofferson's "Me and Bobby McGee," "Little Green Apples," written by Bobby Russell, and later, in the 1980's, "Old Friends," with Ray Price and Willie Nelson. By 1965 and 1966 Miller had won eleven Grammys. In 1965 he was selected as Best Songwriter by the Academy of Country and Western Music and Man of the Year.

Roger Miller. Photo courtesy
the Estate of Roger Miller.

Miller's next big recognition came nearly twenty years later on Broadway for *Big River,* a musical based on Mark Twain's *The Adventures of Huckleberry Finn.* Miller won two Tony Awards for the show, one for Best Musical and one for Outstanding Score. Overall, the show won seven Tonys. Miller was diagnosed with cancer in 1991 and died a year later. He was inducted into the Country Music Hall of Fame in 1995, and his influence can still be seen and heard in a new generation of singers as well as on those who continue to perform his songs. ★

Moon Mullican

Aubrey Wilson Mullican was born in deep East Texas near the Louisiana border on March 29, 1909, and died in Beaumont on January 1, 1967.

He is almost forgotten nowadays, but in his heyday, Moon Mullican was the king of country pianists; in fact he was billed on the *Grand Ole Opry* as "The King of Hillbilly Piano Players." His playing, described by one writer as having merged "swing, blues, honky-tonk, Cajun, ragtime, pop, and country" inspired such piano players as Floyd Cramer, Jerry Lee Lewis, and Mickey Gilley, all of whom admired the music that Moon said was designed to "make the bottles bounce on the tables." Many of Moon's later records are pure rock 'n roll. One example is "Rocket to the Moon."

He learned the boogie-woogie/blues beat from the black musicians who lived near his East Texas home. He grew up on a farm in Polk County, Texas, and heard a good deal of barrel-house piano before he left home at sixteen to play honky-tonk piano in houses of prostitution in the Houston area. His playing of raucous music on the family pump organ, much to the displeasure of his religious family, led to his running away to the big city. Some have suggested that his all-night playing probably earned him the nickname "Moon," others that it came from moonshine whiskey, and a few that he had a moon face and a balding head.

In the late thirties and early forties, Mullican played in and around Houston and Beaumont with Leon "Pappy" Selph's Blue Ridge Playboys, a group that included both Floyd Tillman and Ted Daffan, who wrote the great country hit "Born to Lose" and who became famous with a band called Ted Daffan's Texans, despite the fact that Daffan was from Louisiana. Moon later joined Cliff Burner's Texas Wanderers, a band influenced by the kind of country swing made popular by Milton Brown's Musical Brownies, a group that Bruner had played with before Brown's untimely death in 1936. It was with Bruner that Mullican made his first hit record as a singer with "Truck Driver's Blues." And it was as a member of Bruner's Texas Wanderers that he went to Hollywood and filmed the movie *Village Barn Dance.*

In the 1940s Mullican formed his own band in the Houston area that included the singer Jim Reeves for a while. In the same decade, he joined Jimmie Davis' band and appeared with Davis on Shreveport's KWKH. He wrote songs for Davis' successful campaign for governor of Louisiana in 1944. Later, he wrote songs for Frank Clements, who was governor of Tennessee in the fifties.

Mullican left the various groups he played with in the thirties and forties and became a solo act in 1946. In 1947, he recorded the old Cajun song "New Jole Blon," which sold a million copies, and in 1950, the song he is most remembered for, "I'll Sail My Ship Alone," another million seller. In the fifties, he had hits with Leadbelly's "Goodnight Irene," the ever popular "Mona Lisa," "Sweeter than the Flowers," and his own "Cherokee Boogie." Hank Williams got him on the *Grand Ole Opry* in June of 1951, where he was the only singing piano player on the show. Some commentators have said that Moon is the uncredited co-writer of Hank Williams "Jambalya," one of Hank's biggest all-time hits. Mullican stayed with the *Opry* until 1955.

After he left the *Opry*, Moon played with station KECK in Odessa, Texas, and appeared on Dallas' *Big D Jamboree* and on *Jubilee USA,* a television show on ABC. He toured with many of the stars of the day, both in this country and in Europe. He even made a trip to Vietnam. He made a number of recordings that featured his rock 'n roll piano toward the end of his career. Jerry Lee Lewis was greatly influenced by Moon Mullican's "two-finger" piano style that Moon developed in the days when he was playing in "sporting houses" back in his early career. In a 1966 performance at Fort Worth's Panther Hall, Jerry Lee paid tribute to Moon Mullican as the piano player "who inspired me as a kid in Ferriday." In 1974, Moon Mullican was inducted into the Nashville Songwriters Hall of Fame; many of his albums have been released in recent years. *Moon's Rocks,* (1992), *Moon Mullican: 22 Greatest Hits,* (1994), *The Old Texan: Moon Mullican* (1994), and *Moonshine Jamboree* (2005). ★

Willie Nelson

Willie Hugh Nelson was born April 30, 1933, in Abbott, Texas.

Growing up in a farming community, he later claimed to have been influenced by music all around: from the field hands, both black and Hispanic, from the church, and the local gatherings featuring every genre from Czech polkas to old country tunes. He says he favored Frank Sinatra as a singer. Willie joined the air force but left because of a bad back; he attended Baylor University for one year; and he became a disc jockey in Fort Worth while singing in honky-tonks around the area. By 1956, he had moved to Vancouver, Washington, and from there to Nashville, where he found success as a songwriter but not as a performer. His association with established stars such as Ray Price, Faron Young, Roger Miller, and Patsy Cline left him with unfulfilled ambition, and after his house burned down, as most stories about Willie explain, he decided to move to Austin.

The late 1960s brought Willie Nelson back into many of the taverns and honky-tonks he had played earlier, though after Nashville he developed a different persona and came to epitomize "progressive country," "redneck rock," and "outlaw country" as his fans rediscovered Willie's blends of country, blues, rock, jazz, and gypsy music. Broken Spoke owner James White remembers booking Willie in 1967, and even today Willie might be expected to show up to see some of his friends and play a set with them. The Austin scene caught on to his albums like *Yesterday's Wine, Shotgun Willie, Phases and Stages,* and *Red Headed Stranger* well before those works became national favorites. Willie's Fourth of July picnics, starting with the one in Dripping Springs in 1971 and held intermittently ever since, draw major stars, thousands of fans, and major headaches for the producers in the relentless Texas heat. Willie's shows on the road are full of the standards, beginning with "Whiskey River," usually followed by twenty or so of Willie's songs sprinkled with works by many composers he pays tribute to on a fairly constant basis: Merle Haggard, Ray Price, Lefty Frizzell, Floyd Tillman, Cindy Walker, Bob Wills, and many younger artists. It is common for Willie never to leave the stage during a three-hour set.

Willie Nelson's band has remained a close-knit group since he began playing in Austin. It includes sister Bobbie on piano, Paul English on drums, Bee

Willie Nelson and James White in the sixties. Courtesy of James White.

Spears on bass, Mickey Raphael on harmonica, Jody Payne and Jackie King on guitar, and Bill English, percussion. Sometimes other "family members" such as Freddy Powers, Johnny Gimble, or the late Grady Martin join his regulars. In the 1980s and '90s he performed and recorded with hundreds of his peers and fellow songwriters, including Waylon Jennings, Kris Kristofferson, Dolly Parton, Lee Ann Womack, Brenda Lee, Charlie Walker, Jessi Colter, and Tompall Glaser.

Willie has written over 2,500 songs according to Turk Pipkin, co-author of *The Tao of Willie*. His lyrics combine the imagery and texture of poetry layered with bitterness, loneliness, or sheer joy. He also has an acting career that includes character and starring roles in *The Electric Horseman, The Songwriter, Honeysuckle Rose, Barbarosa, Wag the Dog,* and *The Dukes of Hazzard.* Willie has championed environmental activities with his vegetable-based "Willie Nelson Biodiesel," political issues with his Farm Aid concerts, and support of candidates Kinky Friedman for governor of Texas and

Dennis Kucinich for U.S. president. He has performed in hundreds of fund-raising concerts such as the one for tsunami relief through UNICEF.

The number of albums Willie Nelson has recorded must drive discographers and biographers crazy, because various sources will list between 100 and 250 to date (2007). His awards may be easier to catalogue, with numerous CMA and Academy of Country Music tributes and nine Grammys. He received recognition at the Kennedy Center Honors ceremony in 1998. Needless to say, he is a member of The Texas Country Music Hall of Fame and The Country Music Hall of Fame. His public life and his touring have obviously affected his private life. He married his fourth wife, Ann-Marie D'Angelo, in 1991, while working off a debt to the IRS of $16.7 million, and suffered a bankruptcy proceeding in which many of his possessions were auctioned. Some friends bought them and gave them or loaned them back, as is the supposed case with his golf course, recording studio, and occasional home in the township of Luck, Texas, outside of Austin ("If you ain't here, you're out of luck.") Willie cleared his debt by 1993, partly by release of an album in 1992, the profits of which went directly to the IRS—*The IRS Tapes: Who'll Buy My Memories.*

Willie has never lost his sense of humor nor seemed to be diminished by the demands of his profession. Soon after the release of the movie *Brokeback Mountain,* with Willie on the sound track, he recorded a new version of an old song, "Cowboys

Are Frequently, Secretly Fond of Each Other" (2006). In the first three months of 2007, Willie's tours have taken him to Europe, the southern U.S., across Texas, as well as to Las Vegas, New York, and Washington D.C. He is, as ever, "On the Road Again." ★

Buck Owens

Alvin Edgar Owens, Jr. was born near Sherman, Texas, August 12, 1929, and died in Bakersfield, California on March 25, 2006.

Buck Owens is one of the rare country musicians who ruled the 1960s without attaching himself to Nashville. The odd side of this dominance—fifteen number-one hits in a row—was his long engagement with the television program *Hee Haw,* which diminished rather than enhanced his reputation as a creative force in country music. The cornpone series, which also attracted some outstanding performers, was not to be Owens' downfall, however, since he was rediscovered in the 1990s and achieved almost reverential treatment from an entirely new crop of performers.

Owens was the son of sharecroppers in North Texas. He took his nickname from the family mule, the story goes, at age three. In 1937, the family headed west, following the trail of farmers and ranchers escaping the dust bowl of Oklahoma and Texas. When the family car broke the trailer hitch in Phoenix, the family decided to stay, locating in Mesa. By age thirteen, Owens was through with school and worked as a field hand hauling produce. He says he dreamed of not having to pick cotton and potatoes and not having to be too hot or too cold. To escape a life as a laborer, he began learning musical instruments on his own. First he learned to play a mandolin; then a steel guitar, a sax, a harmonica—whatever the band needed.

Owens packed a lot of action into his late teens and early twenties. He drove a truck, but he also played on local radio shows and met a young singer named Bonnie Campbell, whom he married in 1948. He became impressed with Bakersfield, California, after two uncles told him that farm and oil workers made for a thriving honky-tonk scene where Owens could make a living with his music. He moved there in 1951 and for seven years played at the Blackboard as lead singer and guitar player. The band apparently tried all musical forms to get the dancers dancing: country, rhythm and blues, polkas, and rumbas. He was influenced by Western Swing and the cowboy music he heard on Mexican border radio stations. He played in Bakersfield and in small towns and polished his unique brand of honky-tonk. He was also honing his skills, and playing his Fender Telecaster, doing session work in Los Angeles for the likes of Tennessee Ernie Ford, Sonny James, Wanda Jackson, and Tommy Collins. Collins took Owens with him on tour—to Nashville, even—and Buck later recorded Tommy's "If You Ain't Lovin' You Ain't Livin'," which became a hit for him.

He began to record in the mid-1950s, but nothing clicked. The honky-tonk scene in Bakersfield was sobering up, and he was divorced, then remarried. With rock 'n roll knocking down the country charts, Owens bought an interest in a radio station in Puyallup, Washington, and in 1958 began his career as a disc jockey, sound engineer, and owner. He met the sixteen-year-old Don Rich, who then played fiddle but who later would hammer out the Bakersfield sound that made Owens famous.

While in the radio business, Owens continued to record some of his own songs and some co-written with Harlan Howard. By 1960 he knew he could make it in the recording business, so he left the radio station, moved back to Bakersfield, and persuaded Don Rich to leave college and join him. By this time the "country" sounds of Nashville were layered with strings and

Buck Owens with Lt. Governor Ben Barnes at the Preston Smith/Ben Barnes inaugural celebration on January 21, 1969. Jimmy Dean is on the viewer's right. Courtesy Texas State Library and Archives Commission.

sugared with pop, as we hear in Patsy Cline and Eddy Arnold. Owens had put together a road band that featured solid guitar work up front, with drums, fiddle, and pedal steel, and he countered the Nashville sound with a sharp, honky-tonk beat laced with polka style that he captured on recordings precisely because of what he had learned working in radio. He almost made it with "You're for Me" in 1962, but "Act Naturally" was to be his first number-one hit (later recorded by the Beatles) and the string of hits continued with "My Heart Skips a Beat," "Together Again," "Love's Gonna Live Here," and an instrumental "Buckaroo," the name of his band (given by a short-term bass player named Merle Haggard). These successes led to performances in Carnegie Hall, the London Palladium, and the White House. He had a television program, *Buck Owens Ranch*, which ran for six years even as he was buying more radio stations, a music publishing company, and a recording studio in Bakersfield, the town now tagged by fans "Buckersfield."

Owens said of himself, "I'd like to be remembered as a guy that came along and did his music, did his best, and showed up on time, clean and ready to do the job, wrote a few songs and had a hell of a time." His 1969 to 1986 stint as co-host of *Hee Haw* put him in the national spotlight, but for his part, he kept it country—"no social message—no crusade. It's fun and simple." He was critical of the style and arrangement of many new singers: "assembly-line, robot music turns me off." But he brought both old and newly discovered talent to the immensely popular show. The loss of Don

Rich in an accident in 1974 deeply affected Owens, and many thought his performances suffered. It wasn't until 1988, when Dwight Yoakum appeared on the scene and they took "Streets of Bakersfield" to number one that Owens' career once again surged, going back to the hard-driving sounds of his earlier hits. A member of the Nashville Songwriters Hall of Fame, Buck was elected to the Country Music Hall of Fame in 1996. He died soon after a performance in Bakersfield. The Continental Club in Austin, Texas, holds an annual bash near his birth date in August, and since he once showed up, many think he will again—in some form. ★

Ray Price

Noble Ray Price (listed in the CMA Hall of Fame as Ray Noble Price, but on the Official Web Site as Noble Ray Price) was born in Perryville, Texas, on January 12, 1926.

He served in the U. S. Marine Corps from 1944 until 1946. In 1948, he attended North Texas Agricultural College (now the University of Texas at Arlington) planning to be a veterinarian, but it was not long before he gave up his college career and began singing on Abilene's KRBC, and in 1949 landed a spot on Dallas station KRLD's *Big D Jamboree,* one of the better country venues at the time. Two years later, he was in Nashville, rooming with Hank Williams and touring with his band. He became a member of *The Grand Ole*

Opry in 1952, and, after Williams died in 1953, Price formed his own band, The Cherokee Cowboys, made up of remnants of Hank's Drifting Cowboys. Among the musicians in his band in the early years were Willie Nelson, Roger Miller, and Johnny Paycheck. Other Cherokee Cowboys who went on to stardom were Buddy Emmons, Darrell McCall, and Johnny Bush. Miller wrote one of Price's early hits, "Invitation to the Blues," and Willie Nelson wrote the song that has been a staple in Price's repertoire ever since, "Night Life."

When Ray Price recorded "Crazy Arms" in 1956, it spent twenty weeks as number one and stayed on the charts for forty-five weeks. The Official Ray Price Fan Club says, "Crazy Arms" knocked Elvis Presley off the charts that year. On the "Crazy Arms" recording, Price introduced what has come to be called the "Ray Price Shuffle Beat," a 4/4 beat that has become a feature of country music. *The Encyclopedia of Country Music* says "Crazy Arms" was the turning point in Ray's career. In 1959, "The Same Old Me" went to the top of the charts, and in 1970, his recording of Kris Kristofferson's "For the Good Times" went to the top of the country charts and became number eleven on the pop charts. In the '70s Ray Price had three number-one hits.

When Price recorded "Danny Boy" in 1967, he used a large orchestra and began the trend away from his early "country" sound. "Danny Boy" became a pop hit, as did his album *Prisoner of Love,* recorded with a fifty-piece orchestra in 2000. *Prisoner of Love* includes jazz, pop, country, and blues. Ray sings such songs as

"What a Wonderful World," "Fly Me to the Moon," and Ray Charles' great hit "Ramblin' Rose." His change in style alienated some of his country fans, but except for a few complaints, Ray Price has maintained a strong following among country music fans for most of his career—despite the shift to tuxedos and music with a big band sound.

In 1970, Ray Price won a Grammy and three awards from the Academy of Country Music. He was chosen for Best Album, Best Single, and Best Song. Eight times he was named number-one country and western singer, and won twelve *Billboard* awards. His last number-one hit was "Diamonds in the Stars" in 1982, the year he appeared as a minor singer in Clint Eastwood's movie *Honky-Tonk Man*. In 1996, he was inducted into the Country Music Hall of Fame and in 2001 into the Texas Country Music Hall of Fame.

Ray Price. Courtesy of Ray Price fan club.

He spent part of the 1990s singing in his theater in Branson, Missouri, though he still managed to tour for at least a third of each year. In 2007, he toured all across the country with Merle Haggard and Willie Nelson, backed up by Ray Benson and Asleep at the Wheel. The long tour ended with triumphant sessions in New York, Washington D.C., and *The Grand Ole Opry* in Nashville. The tour album is entitled *The Last of the Breed* and rose to the top of the charts as soon as it appeared. A *New York Times* review said when the three singers performed "it was a summit meeting of honky-tonk singing."

Ray Price has been a star for more than fifty years, an endurance record rare in country music circles. Besides such great hits as "Crazy Arms," "Night Life," "You're the Best Thing that Ever Happened to Me," "Loving You Is Easier," and "Heartaches By the Number," Price has had hits with such classics as "Please Release Me," "Help Me Make It Through the Night,"' and the Bob Wills standards, "San Antonio Rose" and "Faded Love." Rick Koster says in his *Texas Music* (NY: St. Martin's, 1998), that Price songs covered all eventualities: "it wasn't unusual for couples to have danced to Price at their high school proms, during their courting years, at their wedding, and throughout the long slide toward divorce—at which times they'd cue up Price hits like 'Burning Memories' or 'For the Good Times' and weep copious tears into their beer bottles." ★

Jim Reeves

Born James Travis Reeves in the Deadwood Community,
Panola County, Texas, on August 20, 1923
(the Country Music Hall of Fame has him born a year
later, but his birth certificate gives the correct date).
He died in a plane crash on July 31, 1964.

Many biographies have Jim Reeves playing baseball for the University of Texas, but a world authority on Jim Reeves, David Morris, maintains that Reeves never attended the university but signed a contract with the St. Louis Cardinals and played with several farm teams in East Texas before injuring himself in a pick-off play in 1946. In 1947, Reeves was a disc jockey for station KGRI in Henderson, Texas, and began recording with Macy and Abbott, two small record labels in Houston. His first real success came with his song "Mexican Joe," (1953) which got him a job as an announcer and singer on Shreveport's KDKH, home of *The Louisiana Hayride,* the pathway to *The Grand Ole Opry* for many country singers—and also the launching pad for Elvis Presley. In 1955, Reeves' recording of "Bimbo" took him to Nashville where he became a member of the *Opry,* which continued until his death nine years later.

Jim Reeves, unlike most of the *Opry* singers, made his name not as a traditional country singer but as a crooner like Bing Crosby. Leo Jackson, Jim's guitarist, quotes Chet Atkins as saying, "Jim Reeves was the singer Eddie Arnold wished he was." The two songs that made Reeves a country star were "He'll Have to Go" and "Four Walls," both made when he began recording with RCA Victor. "He'll Have to Go" was number one on the country charts and number two on the pop charts. These two songs, and many others, also made Jim Reeves an international star. He toured Europe three times and twice made trips to South Africa, where he was more popular than Elvis and where he filmed the movie *Kimberly Jim*, which was released after his death. According to one source Reeves was so popular among the Zulus that they called him "King Jim." He even sang some of his songs in the Afrikaans language.

Over a relatively brief career, Jim Reeves had ten singles that were number one and four albums that went to the top of the country charts, all four albums in the years after his death. Twenty-one of his singles and nine of his albums made the pop charts, though only one single went as high as number two.

Jim Reeves was a great star in Norway, Sweden, the Netherlands, Germany, as well as in India, where his gospel albums are still played. One of his greatest performances was in Oslo, Norway, just three months before his death, when he was touring with the Anita Kerr Singers, Chet Atkins, and Bobby Bare. The program, filmed by the Norwegian broadcasting network, is still shown in Norway and is available in this country as a compact disc. Jim Reeves was on the pop charts in Norway for sixty-nine weeks. His biggest hit in Norway was "I Love You Because," which was number one for an amazing thirty-nine weeks, followed by "He'll Have to

Jim Reeves. Courtesy of
Jim Reeves fan club.

Go," a top hit for twenty-nine weeks. "Distant Drums," a
song written by Texas songwriter Cindy Walker, went to
number one on the British charts in 1966 and remained
there for forty-five weeks. It was named song of the year
in Britain, a rare accolade for an American "country"
song written by one of the greatest Texas songwriters.

The flourishing Jim Reeves Fan Club in the
Netherlands was founded in 1975 by Arie den Dulk and
Bert Bossink. For the first two years of its existence, its
newsletters appeared only in Dutch, but when the British
Jim Reeves Fan Club closed in 1977, the club began
putting out newsletters in both English and Dutch.

"Gentleman Jim Reeves," unlike so many country
singers, abandoned the western garb so often seen on
the *Opry* and the *Hayride* early in his career. In most
of his photographs, he is shown in tuxedos of various
colors or in tailored coats in bright red or blue. The blue
carries out the motif of his band, The Blue Boys.

Jim Reeves was killed piloting his own tiny Beechcraft Debonair from Batesville, Arkansas, back to his home in Nashville. On August 2, Jim and his pianist/passenger Deane Manuel were found in the wreckage near Brentwood, Tennessee. One possibly unreliable source says the search party included Chet Atkins, Eddy Arnold, Stonewall Jackson, and Ernest Tubb. The funeral was held in Nashville, and the body was then carried to his hometown near Carthage, Texas. There is a large statue of Jim Reeves in Carthage, where he is enshrined as a member of the Texas Country Music Hall of Fame. Reeves was inducted into the Country Music Hall of Fame in Nashville in 1967. His widow, Mary, established the Jim Reeves Museum in Nashville. Mrs. Reeves died in 1999. The couple had no children. ★

Tex Ritter

Woodward Maurice Ritter was born on January 12, 1905, in Murvaul (Panola County), Texas, and died on January 2, 1974, in Nashville, Tennessee.

Tex Ritter started life as Woodward Ritter, but he and the family probably pronounced it "Woodard," which is how he spelled it on occasion. His gravestone in Port Neches has it Woodward. The young Tex moved from Panola County to live with a sister in Nederland, attending South Park High School in Beaumont. As a student at the University of Texas in Austin, Ritter studied under J. Frank Dobie, Oscar Fox, and John A. Lomax, who apparently stimulated his interest in authentic cowboy songs. Ritter did not graduate, although he spent a year in law school and was president of the Men's Glee Club.

He got a job singing cowboy songs on station KPRC in Houston in 1928, and that same year moved to New York where he got a role in the chorus of the operetta *The New Moon.* Ritter left New York to spend a year at Northwestern University in 1929. He was back in New York in 1930 and played the role of the Cowboy in Lynn Riggs' *Green Grow the Lilacs,* the play on which the musical *Oklahoma!* is based. His success in the Riggs play led to his engagement as featured singer in the Madison Square Garden Rodeo in 1932. His next move was to WOR radio and the *Lone Star Rangers,* one of the first western musical broadcasts in New York. In 1936, he signed a movie contract with Grand National, a low-budget company that hoped to pit Ritter against Gene Autry, Roy Rogers, John Wayne, and other singing cowboys.

In five years, Ritter starred in thirty-two movies. He moved from Grand National to Monogram Pictures in 1938. Monogram had slightly better production quality and bigger budgets. He worked with some unknowns and some soon-to-be-knowns in the movies. He appeared with a young Rita Hayworth (billed as Rita Cansino in *Trouble in Texas* (1937). He also played in movies with Robert Mitchum, Bill Elliott, Yakima Canutt, and Russell Hayden. He met and made four movies with the woman who became his wife, Dorothy Fay Southworth. He was with Bob Wills and The Texas Playboys in *Take Me Back to Tulsa* in 1940. He moved to Universal Studios for a Johnny Mack Brown series and ended his movie days with several B-grades from Producers Releasing Corporation. *Flaming Bullets* (1945), was his last movie. Ritter's appreciation of authentic cowboy and country music can often be seen in his movies, and he had record contracts even before leaving for Hollywood with American and later Decca records. In 1942 he signed with Capitol Records and hits soon followed: "Jealous Heart," "Rye Whiskey," "I'm Wastin' My Tears on You," and later, "Have I Told You Lately that I Love You," "Boll Weevil," "Deck of Cards," and "Jingle Jangle Jingle."

Ritter's film days ended after 1945, but he later found another way to get back into the movies. In 1952, *High Noon,* starring Gary Cooper and Grace Kelly, used as its theme Ritter's version of the song "High Noon," ("Do not forsake me, oh my darlin'") which won an academy award for its composer and lyricist. He recorded other music for the movies, but the theme from *High Noon* became his signature song.

"I Dreamed of a Hillbilly Heaven" was a big hit in 1961 and uncovered yet another Ritter talent, that of recitation. In 1953 he joined *Town Hall Party* on television, and later appeared in a series, *Ranch Party,* which ran until 1962. He became president of the Country Music Association in 1963. The Ritters moved to Nashville in 1965 after he had been elected to the Country Music Hall of Fame in 1964, and he began working as co-host with Ralph Emery on a late-night country music show on WSM and appearing as a member of *The Grand Ole Opry*.

Tex Ritter made an unsuccessful bid for the Republican nomination for the U.S. Senate from Tennessee in 1970. Ritter was well respected in Hollywood and Nashville, and his recording and movie status probably moved many of the newly discovered cowboy and southern songs annotated by John A. Lomax into the mainstream of American music. The Tex Ritter Museum is housed in the Texas Country Music Hall of Fame in Carthage, Texas. He also was awarded a star on the Hollywood Walk of Fame. ★

Johnny Rodriguez

Juan Raoul Davis Rodriguez was born on December 10, 1951, in Sabinal, Texas.

Rodriguez is one of country music's enduring stars, having recorded six number-one hits. He rose to fame in the 1970s and 1980s, and in the late 1990s stood trial for murder. He was acquitted in 1999 and has produced some strong albums since his trial.

One source calls him "a Mexican-American country music luminary who walks the line between outlaw country and Texas twang," and his fans call him "Country Music's Classical Crooning Tex-Mex

Legend," but in spite of his roots in South Texas, where contemporaries such as Freddy Fender and Flaco Jimenez dominated the conjunto scene, and, in Fender's case, the Latin rock scene, Rodriguez has maintained a solid country audience for his performances, songwriting, and recordings. He didn't begin as a country singer, but started a high school rock band called The Spocks after the character in the *Star Trek* television series. On his official Web site, he says "My parents favored Latin music, my older brothers country, and my friends rock 'n roll. I liked it all."

In many ways, Johnny Rodriquez has lived the life of a country song. His career as a singer began in jail. He and some friends had been sentenced for stealing and barbecuing a goat, and while he was in jail, a Texas Ranger told promoter Happy Shahan about him, and Shahan put Rodriguez to work at his Alamo Village tourist attraction in Brackettville. While working for Shahan, singers Tom T. Hall and Bobby Bare heard him and arranged for him to visit Nashville. Hall put Johnny in his band, and within a year Rodriguez recorded "I Can't Stop Loving You" and "If I Left It Up to You" for Mercury records.

By 1972, with the release of "Pass Me By," Rodriguez could truthfully carry the label of the first Latin-American country singer and he was named Most Promising Vocalist by the Academy of Country Music. The next year saw two number-one hits, "You Always Come Back (To Hurtin' Me)" and "Ridin' My Thumb to Mexico." He began television appearances and recorded a string of successes in 1975 that hit number-one on the charts: "I Just Can't Get Her out of My Mind," "Just Get Up and Close the Door," and "Love Put a Song in My Heart." Firmly entrenched in Nashville in the 1970s, Rodriguez wrote for others and performed their songs as well. During those years, Johnny Rodriguez was listed among the "Outlaws," and he was able to ride the tag to the end of the decade in a hot new market for country music.

In 1979, Rodriguez signed with Epic records and began being produced by the famous Nashville record man Billy Sherrill. For the next five years, Johnny made a string of top-twenty hits, and his band, The Hole in the Wall Gang, was successful on the concert circuit. In 1983 he had hits with "Foolin'" and "How Could I Love Her So?" But apparently he was dealing with personal problems during the rest of the decade and had only one hit "I Didn't (Every Chance I Had)." He was briefly with Capitol records but changed companies a number of times to less successful labels. He continued to tour, but his popularity faded as he was replaced by a younger generation of singers.

He was in the news in a big and devastating way in 1998 when he was charged with the murder of his friend Israel Borrego. Rodriguez and Borrego had been drinking, and when Johnny heard noises coming from the kitchen, he thought Borrego was an intruder and shot him. Borrego died two hours later in Uvalde. In October of 1999, Rodriguez was acquitted after a seven-day trial when the jurors could not determine the extent of Borrego's intrusion into Johnny's house, although both men were thoroughly intoxicated.

During his career, Johnny Rodriguez has had forty-five singles and twenty-six albums on the country charts. He has a black belt in Tae Kwon Do and is a 2007 inductee into the Texas Country Music Hall of Fame. ★

George Strait

George Harvey Strait was born on
May 18, 1952 in Poteet, Texas.

The singer who more than once would be dismissed by Nashville recording moguls as "too country" with "too much hat" grew up on a ranch in Pearsall, and his working knowledge of ranch life, together with his admiration for singers such as Merle Haggard, Ernest Tubb, and Hank Williams, evolved into a style that still gets classified as hard core country. He says of his early life, "It wasn't exactly a country-music upbringing." Living with his father after his mother departed, Strait remembers that they didn't have a record player in the house, but his father did teach young George to ride horses and rope cows, both skills that have long been a part of his life.

At Pearsall High School Strait played in a garage band. After graduation he enrolled at Texas State University in San Marcos, married his wife Norma, and joined the U.S. Army. While stationed in Hawaii, he began performing with a group called Rambling

Country. His time as lead singer with this service-sponsored group helped hone his voice and his timing. During these years he was greatly influenced by Merle Haggard's performance in the 1970 album tribute to Bob Wills, *The Best Damn Fiddle Player in the World*.

Leaving the army in 1975, the couple tried to stay in Hawaii for a while, but with a new daughter in tow they ran out of money and headed back home to Texas where Strait was enrolled again in the agricultural program at Southwest Texas State University. He posted a notice in San Marcos that he was a singer looking for a band. The Ace in the Hole Band took him on, and they opened at the Cheatham Street Warehouse in San Marcos, and for several years played the South and Central Texas circuits. By 1976 the band had recorded some cuts for a small independent recording company, with several songs written by Strait. But even Strait did not consider them successful. He was invited to Nashville and made some demos which were deemed "too country," and so returned to Texas and college. After earning his degree in 1979 and working at the Hart Ranch in Martindale, Strait thought he had hit the wall with his singing. He took a job in Uvalde with a company that made cattle pens, but Norma, seeing his unhappiness, talked him into giving it one more year in the music business, and Strait gave his notice right away.

Strait made more recordings that didn't get noticed until he met with Erv Woolsey, former owner of the Prairie Rose, where Strait had played a number of times. Woolsey at the time was with MCA Nashville and connected Strait with another producer who helped make some demos, but the response from the studio hierarchy was again "too country." Strait returned to San Marcos to give it another try. This time, his producer friends lured an MCA executive to see Strait in his natural setting, a honky-tonk nightclub. The executive gave Strait one more chance, and the single chosen was "Unwound," which hit the charts in May of 1981 and eventually climbed to number six. Then he recorded a complete album, *Strait Country,* and the hits started coming: "If You Think You Want A Stranger (There's One Coming Home)," "Fool Hearted Memory," "All My Ex's Live In Texas," "Amarillo by Morning," "Does Fort Worth Ever Cross Your Mind" were all on the charts, even though "pop country" was taking hold in Nashville.

Strait embodied the look and sound of a real cowboy, which he was, and performed in stadium and arena settings reaching large audiences. A favorite was the old Astrodome, where for many years he was the featured entertainer. Not many performers could or would enter the arena on a horse at full gallop, slam to a full stop at the edge of the stage, hop off, grab a guitar, and launch into his first song without missing a beat. He can still practice the skills he learned on his father's ranch. Now that his son, George Jr., is old enough to rope and ride, the father and son have both participated in the George Strait Team Roping Classic in San Antonio.

Strait continues to sell more records than almost any other country singer and has thirty-three gold albums to prove it—and sales of sixty-two million. He ventured into videos, which he didn't like, and a movie, *Pure Country,* in which he was cast pretty much as himself.

When Strait won the CMA Male Vocalist of the Year Award in 1986, he dedicated the award to his daughter, Jenifer, who had been killed earlier that year in a car crash. He won CMA Entertainer of the Year award in 1989 and has won eighteen awards from the Academy of Country Music and has been CMA Vocalist of the Year five times. In 2006, he was inducted into the Country Music Hall of Fame, and in 2007, he was ranked as the all-time leader in singles in all formats. He has cut back on his touring, a fact perhaps reflected in his recent album, *The Road Less Traveled.* ★

Hank Thompson

Henry William Thompson was born
September 3, 1925, in Waco, Texas, and died
November 6, 2007, in Fort Worth.

If there could be said to be an anthem for hard-core country music it is "The Wild Side of Life," as recorded in 1952 by Hank Thompson and the Brazos Valley Boys. People who don't know call the song "I Didn't Know God Made Honky-tonk Angels," the key line of the refrain. The song stayed at number one on the C&W charts for three months and was voted the Country Song of the Year.

Hank Thompson had already made a name for himself before "The Wild Side of Life," but that song alone would have made him the star he has been for seven decades. Although he learned the harmonica as a child in Waco, it was after his parents bought him a four-dollar guitar in a secondhand store that he found his musical calling. He learned to play well enough that he was "Hank the Hired Hand" on station WACO during his high school years.

In 1943, he joined the U.S. Navy and served as a radioman until the end of the war. While in San Diego, he persuaded his officers to let him play clubs in the area, and when he was in the South Pacific, he entertained his shipmates and broadcast on some of the military stations aimed at increasing troop morale. Back in the states, he took advantage of navy programs to attend college at Southern Methodist University in Dallas, the University of Texas, and Princeton. He gave some thought to becoming an engineer, but in 1946, he got a job singing on a radio show in Dallas called *Cornbread Matinee*. At about that time, Tex Ritter got him an audition with Capitol Records and Hank's "Whoa, Sailor" and "Humpty Dumpty Heart" became hits in 1946. Now, Hank Thompson and The Brazos Boys were off on an odyssey that led to sales of more than sixty million records over the years. He has had twenty-nine top-ten hits and nineteen that made the top twenty. In 1954 alone, he had five top tens. The band he formed after the war, The Brazos Valley Boys, was voted the best country and western band for fourteen straight years in the 1950s and '60s.

Billed as the King of Western Swing and the King of Honky-tonk Swing, Hank Thompson is one of the most enduring singers and songwriters of his era. He grew up listening to Jimmie Rodgers and Bob Wills and seeing the singing cowboy movies of Gene Autry. His decision to go into the Western Swing genre was certainly influenced by the success of Bob Wills, who was one of the fathers of Western Swing. Hank had a television show on WKY-TV in Oklahoma City from 1954 until 1957 and was one of the first county singers to hit the Las Vegas circuit. His album *Live at the Golden Nugget* appeared in 1960. Two of his sixties hits were "Six Pack to Go," which reached number ten in 1960, and the Woody Guthrie standard, "Oklahoma Hills," which made it to number seven in 1961.

In 1989, Hank Thompson was inducted into the Country Music Hall of Fame, and in 1997, he was made a member of the Nashville Songwriters Hall of Fame. He has more albums than most country singers, and in 1997 released *Hank Thompson and Friends,* which included such singers as George Jones, Kitty Wells, and Lyle Lovett. He has made tribute albums like *Hank Thompson Sings and Plays Bob Wills,* and a music video, *Gotta Sell Them Chickens.* ★

Hank Thompson.
Courtesy of
Hank Thompson.

Ernest Tubb

*Ernest Dale Tubb was born on February 9, 1914, in
Crisp, Texas, and died in Nashville, Tennessee,
on September 6, 1984. He is buried in
Hermitage Gardens, Nashville.*

Considered by many the greatest of the Texas pure
country singers, Ernest Tubb learned the guitar on his
own while working as a soda jerk in San Antonio. He
sang for a while at radio station KONO without pay, and
about this time met Carrie Rodgers, widow of Jimmie
Rodgers, the singer and yodeler that Tubb admired and
imitated. Mrs. Rodgers lent Tubb (affectionately known
as "ET") one of Jimmie's guitars and helped him to a
recording contract with RCA Victor. After he had his
tonsils out and could no longer yodel and hit the high
notes Rodgers was famous for, ET developed the gritty,
gravelly style that made him famous for fifty years.

After several years of poor pay and an undistin-
guished career as "The Gold Chain Troubadour" for a
flour company, ET recorded "I'm Walking the Floor
Over You," a million-selling hit that became his theme
song. This song led to a trip to Hollywood to make several movies with a western theme and, in 1933, a spot
on WSM radio's *The Grand Ole Opry*. ET remained a
regular on the *Opry* for many years and helped many
other performers join that "Mother Church of Country Music."

In 1934, he married Lois Elaine Cook, the
inspiration for his song "Blue Eyed Elaine," which he

Ernest Tubb.
Courtesy of Ernest Tubb.

sang on many of his records. On a duet album, as he and his son Justin sing that song, ET says, "sing it pretty for your mother, son." This was long after he and Elaine had divorced in 1948. In 1949, he married Olene Adams Carter ("My Tennessee Baby"). By that time, Ernest Tubb was one of the biggest names in country music, with appearances on the *Opry*, a killing touring schedule, and a long string of hit songs. He had already had seven songs on the top ten charts, such songs as "Don't Rob Another Man's Castle," "Blue Christmas," Floyd Tillman's great song, "Slipping Around," and "Warm Red Wine."

In a long career, Ernest Tubb recorded more than 250 songs and sold more than thirty million records. He was inducted into the Country Music Hall of Fame in 1965. He was still on the *Opry* and for years had a Friday night program at his Ernest Tubb Record Shop near the Ryman Auditorium in Nashville. His record store program helped such singers as Hank Williams,

Hank Snow, and Loretta Lynn. Helping Loretta Lynn get her career started led to ET playing himself in the movie about her life, *A Coal Miner's Daughter.*

Many music historians credit Ernest Tubb with creating "the honky-tonk sound" by adding electric amplification to his band to help overcome the crowd noise in southern dance halls and beer bars. He was not the first to add amplification, but when he made it a feature of his band, The Texas Troubadours, it became the standard for country music. That honky-tonk sound sold records and attracted people to dance halls from the 1940s on. Tubb's band never varied much in size and always included several guitars, especially a pedal steel played by a succession of artists he named when they took solos. He would finish a chorus and say, "Bashful Billy Byrd," or "and now here's Butterball" or "Little Pete Mitchell." ET sang all the songs himself in that granite baritone that was not always on key. He said, "I don't care if I hit the right note or not. I'm not aiming for perfection—I'm looking for individuality." In a video of his life called *Sing, Troubadour, Sing,* he tells of hearing a patron in a bar listening to one of his songs on the juke box who says to his wife, "Hell, I can sing better than that." ET overheard him and said, "You probably can, brother, you probably can."

But it is unlikely that the bar patron could have made hits with his nephew Talmadge Tubb's "Waltz Across Texas" or some of his signature songs: "Filipino Baby," "There's a Little Bit of Everything in Texas," or "Little Band of Gold." And nobody could stir an audience like ET. He always ended his concerts by singing "Thanks (Thanks a Lot)" and flipping his guitar over to show the "THANKS" he had painted on the back.

Many great country singers have entertained audiences over the last three quarters of a century, but few have had the originality, the depth of feeling, the down-home realism of the late Ernest Tubb. He always made the songs come from the heart, and he always kept them "low to the ground," the motto he always stressed to his band members—"keep it low to the ground, boys, keep it low to the ground." ★

Tanya Tucker

Tanya Denise Tucker was born in Seminole, Texas, on October 10, 1958.

Her father was a construction worker who went where jobs took him, and Tanya grew up mostly in Arizona. At an early age she began showing up in honky-tonks and getting the band to let her sing with them. She remembers haunting the VFW Club in Wilcox, Arizona, and persuading singers like Ernest Tubb and Little Jimmy Dickens to let her sing with their bands. In Phoenix, she appeared on a children's show, and in 1972, after the family moved to Utah, she landed a small part in the Robert Redford movie *Jeremiah Johnson*.

That same year, her father, Beau Tucker, eager to further Tanya's career, moved to Henderson, Nevada, to be close to the Las Vegas entertainment scene. Tanya made homespun demo tapes that went nowhere, but after her father had one professionally done, she landed in Nashville with the legendary producer Billy Sherrill of Capitol records. When he recorded Tanya singing "Delta Dawn," she became an overnight star of country music at thirteen. The song rose to number six on the country charts and even made a small impression on the popular charts.

Within months after "Delta Dawn" became a hit, Tanya—"the Texas Tornado"—was called to the Mother Church of Country Music, *The Grand Ole Opry.* Two years later, Tanya was featured on the cover of *Rolling Stone,* the premier rock publication. In the two years between "Delta Dawn" and the *Rolling Stone* cover, Tanya had a number-one hit with "What's Your Mama's Name" and was banned by a number of stations with her hit "Will You Lay with Me (In a Field of Stone)." During this part of her early career that she was named country music's Top New Vocalist by the Academy of Country Music.

Tanya had more hits once she had signed a big contract with MCA. Her album *Tanya Tucker* featured the number-one country hit "Lizzie and the Rainman." Her "San Antonio Stroll" was a hit on the pop charts as well as on the country charts. In 1978, when she was just twenty, Tanya went to LA and recorded the album *TNT,* which was much more rock than country and which alienated some of her country fans. Nevertheless, the album became a gold record and the country song on it, "Texas (When I Die)" was a number-one hit. It was during this period that she became engaged to Glen Campbell, and the two of them recorded a couple of hits. Her engagement to the two-decades-older Campbell was called off, and Tanya sued him for physical abuse. Tanya had problems with drugs, and her career suffered in the post-Campbell years.

Her 1982 album, *Changes,* had a top-ten hit, but her career languished in the early eighties until her album *Girls Like Me* came out in 1986 and had a top-ten hit and several others that made the charts. In 1988, she checked into the Betty Ford Clinic, and that same year she had some of her best hits: "Just Another Love" went to number one and "One Love at a Time" was number three on the charts. She also had number-one hits in 1988 with "I Won't Take Less Than Your Love," "If It Don't Come Easy," and "Strong Enough to Bend." During these years, Tanya Tucker was all over the tabloids, especially after she gave birth to a child out of wedlock in 1989. Her second child was born in 1991, also out of wedlock, and, while she was in the hospital awaiting the baby, she was named Female Vocalist of the Year. The year before she had been named Female Vocalist of the Year by Country Music Television.

She has not been as successful in the last couple of decades, though she has had a few hits, and she was the half-time entertainer at Super Bowl XXVIII. She wrote her autobiography in 1997 with the interesting title of *Nickel Dreams, My Life.* Tanya Tucker appeared on several episodes of *The Love Boat,* was once on *Fantasy Island,* and made the obligatory visit to *Hee*

Haw. She continues to record, and her 2005 album, *Live at Billy Bob's,* received good reviews. She had a television series, *Tuckerville,* on the History Channel in 2005–06 that ran to seventeen episodes. It was a behind-the-scenes look at her family life. Over a long and tumultuous career, Tanya has had eleven number-one country hits, and was named to the Texas Country Music Hall of Fame in 2003. ★

Don Walser

was born in Brownfield, Texas, on September 14, 1934, and died in Austin, Texas, on September 20, 2006.

Donald Ray Walser grew up in Lamesa, Texas, and, since his mother had died when he was eleven, he spent his afternoons at home alone listening to such country and western performers as Bob Wills, Hank Williams, and Lefty Frizzell. When he was made a National Heritage Fellow in 2000, he said he had listened to singers and yodelers Jimmie Rodgers, Elton Britt, and Slim Whitman, "and when I couldn't find more, I wrote 'A Rolling Stone from Texas' and a few others." By the age of sixteen he had his first band and had begun singing "A Rolling Stone from Texas" and many of the standards of the day—and of a generation past. "A Rolling Stone" became his theme song and was used as the title of his first album, produced by Ray Benson, band leader of Asleep at the Wheel. It was the first of ten albums that Don Walser recorded.

Don Walser joined the Texas National Guard at age fifteen (he said he was seventeen) and remained a member for forty-five years. He married his wife Pat when he was sixteen and remained with her until his death. In one of his great songs, "The Hot Rod Mercury," he calls her Patricia Jane, the name he always used for her. Much of his guard time was spent in West Texas, where he played on weekends at bars, VFW halls, and for fellow servicemen. He recorded "A Rolling Stone from Texas" when he was only eighteen and was playing with a Midland band called The Texas Plainsmen. During those West Texas years, he practiced the yodel he had learned from the Rodgers, Britt, and Whitman records and from some of the yodeling cowboys he had seen in the movies at the Sky-Vue Drive In Theatre in Lamesa.

In 1984, he was transferred to Camp Mabry in Austin, Texas. He had been a mechanic, a supervisor, and an auditor for the guard. He finished his career as auditor for the Adjutant General of the Texas National Guard at Camp Mabry. Once he was in Austin, the hottest country venue in the country in those days, he began playing clubs and drawing admiring crowds for his singing and yodeling. He played at Henry's Bar and Grill on Burnet Road in his first years in Austin, and by the late 1980s was a regular at Austin's famous Broken Spoke. When he retired from the guard, he devoted full time to playing with his Pure Texas Band and recording the ten albums that made him one of the legends of Texas music.

His fame spread beyond Austin and Texas, and in 1999 and again in 2001, he was invited to play at *The Grand Ole Opry*. His albums came out regularly in his last years, and some of his own songs, "A Rolling Stone from Texas," "The John Deere Tractor Song," "Down at the Sky-Vue Drive In," and "The Hot Rod Mercury," became signature songs for Walser and appear on several of his ten albums.

Playboy Magazine called Don Walser "the Pavarotti of the Plains," and the *Austin American-Statesman* called him "the savior of real country music." He appeared on ABC's *Prime Time Live*, NPR's *Austin City Limits*, *All Things Considered*, and *Fresh Air*. The *New Yorker* included a color drawing of Don Walser in their "Goings on About Town" section. In 2000, he performed at the Lincoln Center when the National Endowment for the Arts awarded him The National Heritage Fellowship.

Don Walser was eulogized as a friendly, down-to-earth man who never seemed to realize how famous

Don Walser.
Courtesy
of Don Walser.

he had become. When he was being inducted at Lincoln Center, he refused to be spirited in the side door and insisted on shaking hands with the crowd who had gathered to hear him. Between sets at the Broken Spoke, he sat with Patty Jane and some of his four children and autographed the pictures which he brought with him and provided free to his fans.

His son created a wonderful tribute to Don Walser with recorded songs and a slide show on the Don Walser Web site (http://www.donwalser.com/). ★

About the Authors

PHIL FRY

Phillip L. Fry, a native of Hugo, Oklahoma, has lived in Austin, Texas, for forty years, where he heard all the great country singers. He is an independent scholar with a PhD in English from the University of Texas, where he worked on both *The Handbook of Texas* and *The Handbook of Texas Music.* ★

JIM LEE

James Ward Lee has lived in Texas for almost fifty years, and for all that time has been a fan of country music. Lee is past president and now fellow of the Texas Folklore Society. He is emeritus professor of English at the University of North Texas. He lives in Fort Worth. His latest book is *Adventures with a Texas Humanist.* ★

Texas Country Singers
ISBN 978-0-87565-3655-5
Case. $8.95
A Texas Small Book
★

ISBN 978-0-87565-365-5

9 780875 653655   50895